Penguin Masterstudies

The Tempest

Dr Sandra Clark was educated at Westfield College, University of London. As well as working in publishing she has taught at the University of Toronto and the Open University, and is currently a lecturer in English at Birkbeck College, University of London. She has published on Shakespeare and Elizabethan literature and her first book, *The Elizabethan Pamphleteers. Popular Moralistic Pamphlets 1580–1640*, came out in 1983.

Penguin Masterstudies

Advisory Editors: Stephen Coote
                  Bryan Loughrey

William Shakespeare

The Tempest

Sandra Clark

Penguin Books

For Oliver Clark

Penguin Books Ltd, Harmondsworth, Middlesex, England
Viking Penguin Inc., 40 West 23rd Street, New York, New York 10010, U.S.A.
Penguin Books Australia Ltd, Ringwood, Victoria, Australia
Penguin Books Canada Ltd, 2801 John Street, Markham, Ontario, Canada L3R 1B4
Penguin Books (N.Z.) Ltd, 182–190 Wairau Road, Auckland 10, New Zealand

First published 1986

Made and printed in Great Britain by
Richard Clay (The Chaucer Press) Ltd, Bungay, Suffolk

Filmset in nine on eleven point Monophoto Times by
Northumberland Press Ltd, Gateshead, Tyne and Wear

All references to *The Tempest* follow the New Penguin Shakespeare edition,
edited by Anne Righter.

Contents

'The Tempest' as a 'last' play

The Tempest was first published in the 1623 Folio of Shakespeare's plays. Although there have in the past been a variety of views as to when it was written, and it has sometimes been regarded as one of Shakespeare's earliest works, there is now clear and generally accepted evidence for a date between late 1610 and November 1611. The earlier date is established by the fact that Shakespeare used for his play several pamphlets describing a colonizing expedition to Virginia in 1609; these were published late in 1610, with one exception, *A True Reportory of the Wracke and Redemption of Sir Thomas Gates, Knight*, by William Strachey, which did not in fact appear in print until 1625, though Shakespeare must have read it in manuscript. A performance of the play, probably its first at court, is recorded in the Accounts of the Revels on Hallowmas Night, 1 November 1611, so that the available time-span for its composition is clearly demarcated. It may have been that the interest aroused by the Virginia expedition gave Shakespeare the initial stimulus to write *The Tempest*, but it is evident from the connections between this play and his other late works that he had been thinking along these lines for some time.

This dating makes *The Tempest* Shakespeare's last complete play, although he did not, as is sometimes supposed, retire from the theatre completely after writing it. He went on to collaborate with the successful young playwright John Fletcher on *Henry VIII* and *The Two Noble Kinsmen* in 1613, and made his last recorded appearance in London in November 1614 after which he passed the remainder of his life in Stratford.

There have often been attempts to claim one or other of Shakespeare's romances as an early play, but modern opinion generally takes the view that *Cymbeline*, *The Winter's Tale*, *The Tempest* and the Shakespearean parts of *Pericles* were all written towards the end of Shakespeare's professional career over a period of about three years without other plays intervening. These plays have more in common than any other group of his plays. *The Tempest* is the last and, many would say, the finest of the four.

Shakespeare's theatrical career was not long in years, but it encompassed astonishing development, and the romances are plays which could only have been written at the end of it. After the storm and violence of the tragedies, the despair of *King Lear*, the disillusion of *Timon of Athens*, comes this group of pastoral romances, which appear in this context like a vision of hope sprung from inner turmoil. The world of these plays is not without evil – the murderous hate of Dionyza for Marina, the bitter misogyny of Posthumus, Leontes' jealous rage, and the drunkenness, lust and treachery we see in *The Tempest* – but evil never triumphs over goodness. In fact vitality overcomes spiritual desolation and life conquers death in so many instances that it is tempting to interpret the romances as versions of a myth of resurrection. In *Pericles*, Thaisa miraculously survives the storm and the virgin Marina the brothel; in *Cymbeline* Imogen is not really dead though Guiderius and Arviragus sing a poignant lament for the loss of 'golden lads and girls'; in *The Winter's Tale* Hermione, secretly preserved for sixteen years, is at last restored to Leontes, and the lost Perdita comes back to rejuvenate the grieving kingdom of Sicilia; in *The Tempest* Ferdinand and his father are restored to one another, and Prospero gets back his lost throne. The gods are benevolent and look down from heaven to pour their graces on the heads of mortals; each play concludes with the finding of what is lost, the celebration of a young couple's union, the reconciliation of enemies, the reunion of parted kinsfolk. 'Pardon's the word to all' (*Cymbeline*, V.5.420). For Wilson Knight these works represent 'the inevitable development of the questioning, the pain, the profundity, and the grandeur of the plays they succeed' (*The Crown of Life*, p. 9).

Of course, the plays differ in particularities and emphasis, but their similarities are not only in the broadest outlines. All show typical features of the romance mode: situations characterized by qualities of the unlikely, the improbable, the mysterious, the miraculous; distant, exotic locations, with connotations of the Hellenistic pastoral and Arcadian golden-age countryside; long journeys, often by sea, often attended by storm and shipwreck; themes of loss and recovery, exile and return. It has been thought that the improbabilities of Shakespeare's plots resulted from a failure of art or at least a declining interest in craftsmanship, that he was at this time, in Lytton Strachey's notorious words, 'bored with drama, bored, in fact, with everything except poetry and poetical dreams'. But in truth the improbabilities stem from Shakespeare's sense of what is appropriate to the fairy-tale atmosphere of the stories, where realism and verisimilitude are replaced by a different kind of truth, better expressed in symbolic terms. Sometimes Shakespeare even seems to use his improbabilities to draw attention to the fact that his play is a play and not a slice of life. For instance, a minor character in *The Winter's Tale*, describing the circumstances in which King Leontes recovers his long-lost daughter Perdita, is made to say that the story is 'so like an old tale that the verity of it is in strong suspicion' (V.2.28).

In his earlier comedies Shakespeare had always shown a preference for the unlikely or impossible over the realistic, and had never hesitated to make use of coincidence in his plots. In the romances these elements are conspicuously present, though here their effect is not comic or farcical, but rather wonderful and miraculous, an expression of providential design behind the muddles and mistakes of human life. In each play there is a basic story-line, differently treated, but always revolving around the separation and, after much time and suffering, the reconciliation of kinsfolk.

In *Pericles*, this story takes up the last three acts of the play and has the father and husband, Pericles, as its central character. In Act III, Scene 1, he loses his wife Thaisa, apparently dead in childbirth at sea, and is then separated from his baby daughter Marina, when he leaves her with the Governor of Tarsus while he returns to Ephesus. The three of them are not reunited till long after, when Marina has grown up. In *Cymbeline* the focus shifts to the daughter, Imogen, who is a mature woman and a wife. Early on in the play she is estranged from her father who disapproves of her marriage, and later, by a trick, from her husband. At the end, not only are the father and his daughter and her husband reunited, but also two long lost sons of Cymbeline, separated from their family since childhood, are found and restored to their father and sister. The last scene of this play is the most complete vision of family harmony and reconciliation in the romances.

The mood of *The Winter's Tale* and its treatment of a family rift are quite different. Leontes falsely accuses his wife Hermione of infidelity, and she appears to die of grief. The audience is not shown the 'dead' wife secretly preserved, as in *Pericles*, and no hint is given until the last scene of the play that she is really alive. Leontes' ill-founded jealousy causes his separation from his baby daughter Perdita, who, abandoned to die by her father, grows to maturity in another country, and his total loss of his young son Mamillius who dies of grief. Leontes, Hermione and Perdita are reunited after a sixteen-year separation; the restoration of wife to husband takes place in an atmosphere of wonder and miracle, but in this play there is no evading the elements of irrecoverable loss in the story. Husband and wife are now older, some of their best years have been wasted, and they have lost their only son. The ending sounds a note of imperfect consolation not found earlier.

In *The Tempest*, there are divisions within the two families which are never entirely healed: Alonso regains his son Ferdinand whom he had thought drowned, but his daughter Claribel remains in her husband's country of Tunis, 'ten leagues beyond man's life'; and Prospero's reunion with the brother who treated him so treacherously twelve years earlier is not entirely happy. In encouraging the match between Ferdinand and Miranda from behind the scenes, Prospero is more aware of the inevitability of the young girl's independent move towards establishing a new family unit of her own than of her bringing another member into his own circle.

The span in which children grow to maturity is in each case an element in the time-scheme and structure of the play. In *Pericles* and *The Winter's Tale* the action takes place over this period, and a new generation is born while its parents mature in the course of the play. Those plays inevitably fall into two halves, with a long gap of time between the third and fourth acts when the heroine grows up. The fifteen years covered in *Pericles* is not just a generation but also a lifetime; the play begins with Pericles the young man seeking a bride and ends with him as a father preparing to give away his daughter in marriage. The actor must mature and age in view of the audience; but his enactment of ageing is made easier by the deliberately non-realistic presentation of his voyages and tribulations and the fairy-tale style of Gower's narratives. In *The Winter's Tale* the 'great gap of time' in which Perdita grows to adolescence in pastoral Bohemia is subsumed in a single speech of the personified Time:

> *Impute it not a crime*
> *To me or my swift passage that I slide*
> *O'er sixteen years . . .*

(IV.1.4–6)

In *Cymbeline* and *The Tempest*, the generational theme is differently handled. These plays open when all characters are mature, at a moment significantly related to past events in the life of the family. In *Cymbeline* this is twenty years after Cymbeline's sons were snatched from their nursery; in *The Tempest* it is twelve years since Prospero and the infant Miranda were forced into exile from Milan. But apart from this feature, *Cymbeline* and *The Tempest* are very different in their management of time within the play, *The Tempest* with its four-hour time-span being, for Shakespeare, uniquely compact and compressed in this respect.

Scenes of family reunion end each play, though the emotional temperature is much the coolest in *The Tempest*; in the other three, families come together after long and painful separations, and there is great joy and wonderment and a sense of endurance rewarded. Pericles and Leontes are restored to their full identities as husbands and fathers, Cymbeline gets back two sons he had thought long dead, as well as regaining the affections of his daughter and courtiers, and he, like Leontes, makes due reparation for the wrongs he has done to others. In *The Tempest* the motifs of parent–child reunion and of the father's penitence for his misdeeds are present, but subordinate, in the relationship of Alonso and Ferdinand. The theme of the recovery through the benevolence of providence of what has been lost is put into the mouth of Gonzalo in the last scene:

> *Was Milan thrust from Milan that his issue*
> *Should become kings of Naples? O, rejoice*
> *Beyond a common joy, and set it down*
> *With gold on lasting pillars. In one voyage*
> *Did Claribel her husband find at Tunis,*
> *And Ferdinand her brother found a wife*
> *Where he himself was lost; Prospero his dukedom*
> *In a poor isle, and all of us ourselves*
> *When no man was his own.*

(V.1.205–13)

It is a beautiful and even magisterial speech, but its tone does not reflect that of the whole scene with total accuracy. It is the partial perception of 'the good old lord Gonzalo', and does not account for such other parts of the picture as the silence of Antonio who has no words of penitence or joy, or the grotesque antics of Caliban and his confederates. The focus of the scene is less clear than its equivalents in the other three plays, and Prospero stands in a quite different relation to the situation from that of Pericles, Cymbeline or Leontes.

An important element in each of the four plays is the treatment of magic and the supernatural. In *Pericles* a distinction is drawn between the supernatural as such, which occurs in the appearance to Pericles of the goddess Diana, preceded by the sound of the music of the spheres, and natural magic, as demonstrated by Cerimon's ability to restore to life the apparently drowned Thaisa. Only Pericles hears the music which sounds at the moment of his reunion with Marina, and betokens an instance of happiness so pure as to confer on him momentarily a condition of pre-lapsarian innocence. Soon afterwards Diana appears to him in a vision, with a message for his ears alone. By contrast, Cerimon is known in Ephesus as a philanthropist and a practitioner of natural magic; with his experience of 'the disturbances/that nature works, and/... her cures', and with the aid of music, he is able to bring back to Thaisa 'the fire of life'. He is someone 'through whom the gods have shown their power' (V.3.60), but, like Prospero, a mortal man who has acquired his skills through learning and devotion and not a supernatural being. Cerimon has no equivalent in *Cymbeline*, but Pericles' vision of Diana is paralleled by the

11

vision that comes to Posthumus as he lies asleep in his prison cell, when both he and the audience are reassured, albeit at the eleventh hour, of a happy ending to the by now very complicated plot.

In *The Winter's Tale*, as in the earlier two plays, the presiding deity, Apollo, is Hellenistic; he does not appear, but vouchsafes his oracle to the messengers of Leontes to pronounce on the state of Leontes' kingdom. As in *Cymbeline*, the truth of the pronouncement becomes apparent only in the play's final scene, and acts as a means of reassuring the audience, retrospectively, that a benevolent power has been at work all the time. Something of Cerimon's function is to be found in Paulina, who is similarly responsible for preserving the abandoned wife and restoring her at the appropriate moment to her husband. Paulina's methods are mysterious enough to require some disclaimer of witchcraft:

> ... If you can behold it,
> I'll make the statue move indeed, descend
> And take you by the hand: but then you'll think –
> Which I protest against – I am assisted
> By wicked powers.

(V.3.87–91)

But the 'spell' she has used is not a magical one, and she is in no way a learned practitioner like Cerimon, or his more significant descendant, Prospero. Prospero's magical powers shape and control the whole action of *The Tempest*; he is assisted by Ariel and Caliban, and he has a number of spirits at his command, some of whom enact a betrothal masque for Ferdinand and Miranda, taking the parts of Juno, Ceres, and Iris. Supernatural control is exercised not by gods like Diana or Jupiter and Apollo from outside the main action of the play, but by one of the characters, and it is at Prospero's own instigation, in collusion with 'bountiful Fortune, now my dear lady', that the events of the play take place. Hence the effect of a power greater than human, working in the long term for providential ends, is present in the play without Shakespeare's having recourse to scenes of oracles or visions of supernatural beings, although of course it is important to be aware that Prospero is not a god and his control over events is far from total.

In all of these plays Shakespeare has refrained from setting his action in a consistently presented and recognizable historical time so that he has more freedom in dealing with the framework of religious belief within which the characters' spiritual lives take place. Issues of religious belief and of the nature of the moral universe are never explicitly the subject of dialogue as they are, for instance, in *King Lear*, but none the less the plays have a distinctly religious or visionary quality, and the relationship between the natural world of human life on earth and the supernatural world of those divinities which shape our ends (*Hamlet*) is an underlying theme throughout.

The conception of human life gaining meaning from its wider context is explored through the treatment of generations and the cycle of human (and in *The Winter's Tale* seasonal) reproduction. *Pericles* gives the fullest presentation of the life-cycle of an individual, as Pericles himself progresses from young manhood to marriage to fatherhood and to premature old age in well-defined stages. The play also gives the clearest expression to the idea of generational renewal, when Pericles calls his newly-discovered daughter 'Thou that beget'st him that did thee beget' (V.1.196). Daughters are important figures of renewal in each of these plays, but in *Pericles* and *The Winter's Tale* the pattern by which the daughter, who is compared with or mistaken for a goddess in her youth, freshness, and purity, brings about the regeneration of her suffering father is most clearly traced. Before he knows her identity Leontes greets Perdita, 'Welcome hither as is the spring to th' earth'. Seasonal images pervade *The Winter's Tale*, and Perdita's associations with flowers and with the summer festival of sheep-shearing imply her power to restore fertility to her father's winter-bound and childless kingdom. In *Cymbeline* the disguised Imogen is so miraculously beautiful to her brothers that they think her a fairy or an angel, 'divineness no older than a boy'. Miranda in *The Tempest* has also a rare and extraordinary enchantment that makes others take her for a supernatural being; Ferdinand is not at first quite sure if she is mortal, and his father calls her 'the goddess that hath sever'd us,/And brought us thus together'. Her extreme innocence is emphasized; and perhaps Prospero's strong stress on the need for Ferdinand to observe pre-marital abstinence relates to the idea that virginity itself is a magical attribute, and that it is this which guarantees the perpetuation of the true family line. 'Long continuance, and increasing' are amongst the wishes expressed by the spirits in the betrothal masque for Ferdinand and Miranda; and although the heroines of the romances are all childless, three of them virgins, the endings of the plays look towards spousals and new generations.

Another way in which the romances explore the subject of the wider significance of human life is through symbolism, in particular through the symbols of the sea, tempests and music. Sea journeys bring both destruction and joy; they separate kinsfolk and bring travellers near to death, but those who entrust themselves to the elemental and mysterious power of the waves, like Pericles, or Florizel and Perdita in *The Winter's*

Tale, are eventually rewarded by being restored to their families. Journeys by sea are a means of representing both the passing of time and the dangerous uncertainties of life. In Shakespeare's time they were slow and risky, not to be undertaken lightly. He may not have attended very closely to the accuracy of his geographical details (he even on occasion sent characters on sea voyages between two places on the same piece of land, as for instance in *The Two Gentlemen of Verona*), but he was clearly profoundly moved by the idea of the 'watery empire' (*Pericles*) and its mystery. While sea travel can stand for growth and maturing, death by drowning may symbolize spiritual rebirth. The 'sea-change' of which Ariel sings to Ferdinand in *The Tempest* (misleadingly, as it turns out, because Ferdinand's father is not dead) seems to represent the spiritual transformation which can only come about after great suffering and pain. The courtiers, amazed to have survived the shipwreck, find their clothing to be as fresh as when it was first put on. In *Pericles* and *The Tempest* where characters are miraculously saved from drowning in storms at sea, the survival of Pericles, Thaisa, the baby Marina, of Prospero and Miranda, sent to sea by Antonio in 'a rotten carcass of a boat', and of Alonso and the other courtiers, represents movingly the power of life over death, of the human spirit over the worst that the unleashed forces of nature have to offer.

Music is also a symbol with strong connotations of life miraculously retrieved from death, and harmony restored; Wilson Knight calls it 'Shakespeare's normal dramatic antithesis to tempestuous death' (*The Crown of Life*, p. 56). In *Pericles* and in *The Winter's Tale* the supposedly dead women Thaisa and Hermione are returned to life to the sounds of solemn music; in each case the music is much more than accompaniment, and is called for by Cerimon and Paulina respectively as if it were a necessary agent in the restoration. 'Music, awake her, strike!' commands Paulina. In *The Tempest* music is all-pervasive, from the first song with which Ariel lures Ferdinand and allays his passions, to the last in which he sings of freedom and summer days to come; it tricks the clowns and comforts Ferdinand, wakens Gonzalo in time to prevent murder, astounds Alonso with harmony, and fills the mind of Caliban with a vision of rapturous beauty. The dainty spirit Ariel seems himself almost to embody the idea of music, magical and insubstantial.

Music and song form an important part of the spectacular element in these plays, which is most prominent in *The Tempest* but present to differing degrees in all of them. In *Pericles* and *Cymbeline* the most spectacular scenes are those involving the gods and their appearance to the human characters towards the close of each play; in *Cymbeline* this takes the form of a dream-vision coming to Posthumus as he lies asleep in prison, in which the ghosts of his ancestors appear to the sounds of solemn music and Jupiter descends, presumably by means of suspension gear, seated on an eagle, while thunder and lightning play around him. Spectacle in *The Winter's Tale* is both human and divine; the sheep-shearing feast at which Perdita presides celebrates the riches of the summer countryside, and attracts not only country neighbours and friends who dance and make merry, but also passing strangers, and the pedlar Autolycus who delights the country girls with his ribbons and laces and also sells them the latest ballads. By contrast with the natural spontaneity of the music and dancing in this scene, the spectacle of the final scene in which Paulina restores Hermione to Leontes is solemn, closely supervised, carefully timed; here, although no god appears, a divine mystery is present. In *The Tempest* the spectacle is supernatural but always directed and controlled by Prospero: the strange banquet that appears to Alonso and the courtiers and then vanishes when Ariel comes on as a harpy; the spirits in the shape of hounds who chase Caliban, Stephano and Trinculo; and the betrothal masque presented for the entertainment of Ferdinand and Miranda – all these manifestations are contrived by Prospero with the help of Ariel and some of his 'meaner fellows'. Ariel is an actor in many of what we may properly call Prospero's shows, and his fellow-spirits, referred to by Prospero as his 'quality', a contemporary term for the acting profession, appear in 'urchin-shows', as apes and hunting-dogs, and as goddesses or shepherds in the masque. Spectacle in *The Tempest* is much more thoroughly integrated into the play's fabric than in the other romances, and forms a part of the play's meaning. Prospero 'manages' all the action, from the tempest itself, which he calls a 'spectacle', to the general reunion in the last scene; but for all his power he recognizes that life on earth is like a theatre of illusion:

> Our revels now are ended. These our actors,
> As I foretold you, were all spirits, and
> Are melted into air, into thin air; . . .

> . . . We are such stuff
> As dreams are made on; and our little life
> Is rounded with a sleep.

(IV.1.148–50; 156–8)

In this last play Shakespeare poignantly celebrates the beauty of the transitory and ephemeral. Ben Jonson in his wedding masque *Hymenaei*

15

(1606), perhaps an influence on *The Tempest*, lamented that the uniquely perfect beauty of music and spectacle could not be repeated or recaptured:

Only the envie was, that it lasted not still, or (now is past) cannot by imagination, much less description, be recovered to a part of that spirit it had in the gliding by.

(Jonson, *Works*, ed. Herford and Simpson, VII, 224)

All four romances utilize spectacle, but it is only in *The Tempest* that attention is drawn to the means by which the spectacle is produced or to the spectacle as an end in itself. The idea of life like a theatrical show, based on illusion, insubstantial, quickly over, is balanced against the idea of generational cycles and the repeated rhythms of death and renewal. Time and again, a comparison of *The Tempest* with the other last plays shows it standing alone and enigmatic, endlessly productive of meanings and open to many interpretations – like Ariel, 'correspondent to command'.

'The Tempest' as recapitulation

Although *The Tempest* has a very special relationship with the other late plays that immediately precede it, it can profitably be related to a whole range of plays from all stages of Shakespeare's dramatic career. In it, Shakespeare recapitulates and reworks themes and dramatic motifs from both tragedies and comedies, but the effect is never that of patchwork; Shakespeare never merely borrowed or repeated, even from his own work, but always renewed. And such is the unifying effect of *The Tempest*'s peculiar magic and all the diverse materials that went into the making of the play that recapitulations of earlier works may be said to undergo a metamorphosis like that of the drowned king of Ariel's song:

> *Nothing of him that doth fade,*
> *But doth suffer a sea-change*
> *Into something rich and strange.*

(I.2.400–402)

Elements from one of Shakespeare's earliest plays, perhaps even his first, *The Comedy of Errors*, can be discovered, transformed, in *The Tempest* – in particular the primary motifs of the separation of kinsfolk in a storm at sea, and their reunion on a foreign shore some time later. In the city of Ephesus, where all the action in *The Comedy of Errors* takes place, the two pairs of twin brothers Antipholus and Dromio find each other after being separated twenty-three years earlier and the Antipholus brothers are also reunited with their father, and, by amazing coincidence, their mother too. As in *The Tempest*, the time-span of the play is limited. According to one of those irrationally harsh laws which often spark off the action of a comedy, the father, Aegeon, who has just arrived in Ephesus, must pay a fine of one thousand marks by sunset or be executed, because he is from Syracuse, a city at war with Ephesus. So the action of the play covers a natural day, and concludes, happily for all, at sunset. Although the mood is quite different from that of *The Tempest* in its farcical comedy, none the less the play's atmosphere is created from some of the same ingredients: magic, hallucination, doubts about identity, and the background of storm and shipwreck. This combination recurs in a later comedy, *Twelfth Night*. In this play Viola is parted from her twin brother Sebastian at sea, and arrives on the shores of Illyria believing him drowned; again there is an atmosphere of uncertainty and enchantment in which both twins doubt for a time their own identity before confusion is happily resolved. *Twelfth Night* does not deal particularly fully with the relationships of parents and children, but its final scene, where kinsfolk are reunited and what has been lost is found, has hints of what is to come in the romances. In all three plays, the sea forms an ever-present background to the action, a symbol for what is strange and fortuitous in human life.

The comedy most like *The Tempest* is of course *A Midsummer Night's Dream*, and their similarity has long been recognized. One of Shakespeare's eighteenth-century editors, William Warburton, writing at a time when the chronology of Shakespeare's plays was differently regarded, remarked:

> *These first two plays, 'The Tempest' and 'A Midsummer Night's Dream', are the noblest efforts of that sublime and amazing imagination, peculiar to Shakespear* [sic], *which soars above the Bounds of Nature without forsaking sense: or, more properly, carries Nature along with him beyond her established limits.*
>
> (*The Works of Shakespeare*, Vol. 1, p. 3)

The creation of a magical world, based in a natural setting (wood or island) but peopled by supernatural as well as human characters, is common to both plays, and the relationship of Prospero and Ariel is analogous to that of Oberon and Puck. Ariel and Puck, both airy spirits with marvellous powers of motion and self-transformation, are subject to their more potent masters, and act as agents of their projects. In both cases, the spirit-servants modify their masters' plans beneficially, Puck by accident, when Bottom, whom he has translated into an ass, turns out to be the next thing Titania casts eyes upon, and Ariel by sensitive empathy with human feeling, when he urges Prospero to take pity on his enemies. Oberon and Prospero, though one is a spirit and the other a human being, have extensive powers over the forces of nature and are also able to manipulate human beings. Oberon's control over events in the wood outside Athens is less than Prospero's over his island, since in *A Midsummer Night's Dream* the lovers and the rustics have entered the wood of their own volition, whereas in *The Tempest* Prospero has raised the storm that has shipwrecked his enemies on his island, but each character functions in his play like a director, watching over the action and organizing it to suit his own ends. So in each case, the structure of the action has the effect of a play-within-a-play, where the outer layer consists in the machinations of Oberon and Puck, or Prospero and Ariel, and the inner layer of the activities of those characters whom they manipulate like marionettes. Thus Oberon, and to a much greater extent Prospero, are a stage nearer to the audience in awareness and 'reality' than, say, Helena and Demetrius are in *A Midsummer Night's Dream* or Alonso and Ferdinand in *The Tempest*. In each play the effect of layer upon layer of reality is further compounded by the insertion of yet another play-within-the-play – in *A Midsummer Night's Dream* the rustics' performance of the farcical tragedy of Pyramus and Thisbe, in *The Tempest* the wedding masque – so that the audience in the theatre finds itself watching Oberon, or Prospero, who is also watching other characters in the play themselves performing a play. Shakespeare's concern with the nature of theatrical illusion is central to both works, and is used to question the nature of reality. It is no accident that each ends with a speech by a major character exploring the meaning of theatrical art. In *A Midsummer Night's Dream* Puck addresses the audience in the epilogue:

> *If we shadows have offended*
> *Think but this, and all is mended,*
> *That you have but slumber'd here*
> *While these visions did appear,*
> *And this weak and idle theme*
> *No more yielding but a dream.*

(V.1.409–14)

On one level the lines say that just as the actors are 'shadows' so their play in relation to life is like a dream; but on another, there is the implication that there is no real distinction between dreaming and reality. In *The Tempest* Prospero takes these ideas a stage further in his speech to Ferdinand after the disruption of the masque ('Our revels now are ended'), in which he suggests that life itself is an illusion as gorgeous and as lacking in real substance as the 'baseless fabric' of the vision he and his spirits have conjured up. In the Epilogue he steps outside his role in the play and presents himself to the audience as an actor whose existence depends for its meaning on the audience's collusion. The play will have failed unless the audience sanctions it by their applause.

The two plays are closely linked in their treatment of other characteristically Shakespearean concerns, especially the themes of dream and waking or illusion and reality. The experiences undergone by the young lovers in *A Midsummer Night's Dream* under the influence of Oberon's magic love-juice, or those of the shipwrecked courtiers in *The Tempest*, led astray by the strange properties of the island and mystified by the power of Ariel's music, seem like hallucinations or fantasies:

19

> *Methinks I see these things with parted eye,*
> *When everything seems double . . .*
>
> (*A Midsummer Night's Dream* IV.1.187)

says the bewildered Hermia, and Gonzalo, baffled at the sight of Prospero in his robes as Duke of Milan, is equally unable to trust the evidence of his senses: 'Whether this be/Or be not, I'll not swear' (*The Tempest* V.1.122–3). Yet those changes which have been brought about by magical power have permanent and lasting effect: the love-entanglements of Hermia, Helena, Lysander and Demetrius are sorted out, the marital harmony of Oberon and Titania restored, Alonso recognizes and repents of the evil done to Prospero, and Ferdinand is brought to Miranda. Magic may sometimes have its equivocal side, in Puck's mischief and, more seriously, in the black arts of Caliban's mother Sycorax, and Prospero's ability to curse and torment his enemies as well as to bless his friends; but in these plays the ultimate effects of magic are good and beneficial ones, and Shakespeare leaves us in no doubt that there are benevolent powers available to regulate human affairs.

The Tempest also has affinities with some of Shakespeare's tragedies. Sibling rivalry, and the ousting of a good brother by a bad and unscrupulous one, the basis of the situation of Prospero and Antonio, is explored more thoroughly in *Hamlet*, and particularly in *King Lear*, where the theme is presented twice, in Cordelia and her sisters and in Edgar and Edmund. Prospero's bitterness towards the treacherous Antonio, and his image of a creeping poison ('the ivy which had hid my princely trunk,/And sucked my verdure out on't'), perhaps echo the Ghost's account to Hamlet of the behaviour of Claudius: 'The serpent that did sting thy father's life/Now wears his crown'. The more general motif of the exploitation of a good and trusting nature by a treacherous one connects *The Tempest* with *Macbeth*, and in the scene where Antonio persuades Sebastian to make an attempt on the life of the sleeping Alonso there is not only a general resemblance to, but also specific verbal reminiscences of, the build-up to Duncan's murder. Antonio's whole attitude towards conscience and his scornful dismissal of possible hazards of the venture strongly recall Lady Macbeth. There are also other suggestive links between the two plays. The evil earth-magic of Sycorax, a 'damned witch' banished from civilized society for her wicked practices, whose spells and charms – 'toads, beetles, bats' – are recalled by Caliban, bears resemblances to the magic of the witches in *Macbeth* who use such creatures in their conjuring, though Sycorax is credited with both stronger and more objectively quantifiable powers than theirs. Another connection is the symbolic use of the interrupted feast. This is more fully elaborated in *Macbeth*, where the tyrannous Macbeth's first banquet as king begins as a solemn ceremony with each guest in his place and Macbeth ritually playing 'the humble host', but breaks up in 'most admired disorder' when the bloody ghost of murdered Banquo takes its seat, ironically an invited guest, but a hideously unwelcome presence. In *The Tempest* Alonso and the courtiers are lured by the appearance of a mysterious fairy banquet presented to them by spirits in strange shapes and accompanied by 'marvellous sweet music'; to the tired and desperate men this image of civilized society and the 'gentle' manners of the spirits are intensely alluring, but, as in *Macbeth*, the appearance of order is not the reality, and the feast vanishes before their eyes. In *Timon of Athens*, too, the broken feast in Act III, Scene 5, represents the ideal of social order and harmony, spoiled by man's inhumanity to man, in the scene where Timon invites his false friends to dine and exposes their pretensions to warmth and generosity in a banquet of hot water.

But of all the tragedies, it is *King Lear* which has most in common with *The Tempest*. The theme of man's inhumanity to man, expressed at its most intense in the unnatural enmity between siblings or parents and children, is fully explored in *King Lear*, where the unkindness of kinsfolk is deeply felt and suffered but always seen as incomprehensibly cruel. Kent's words, 'It is the stars, the stars above us, govern our conditions', demonstrate the human inability to rationalize what seems to be a failure in nature. 'Twas this flesh begot these pelican daughters', cries Lear bitterly, and the knowledge drives him mad; it is literally beyond reason. In *The Tempest* Prospero has been profoundly hurt by the treachery of Antonio and subsequently disgusted by Caliban's betrayal of trust in misusing his intimacy with Miranda to attempt rape; neither nature nor nurture has proved worthy of trust, and in consequence Prospero has grown bitter and isolated, uncertain even of Miranda's affection and Ferdinand's ability to keep a promise. It takes the empathetic prompting of the spirit Ariel, who though he has no feelings himself, knows what they ought to be, to restore Prospero's human warmth:

ARIEL: *Your charm so strongly works 'em*
               That if you now beheld them your affections
               Would become tender.
PROSPERO: *Dost thou think so, spirit?*
ARIEL: *Mine would, sir, were I human.*
PROSPERO: *And mine shall.*

                                          (V.1.17–20)

But forgiveness cannot work magic, even here; Antonio is given no word of response to Prospero's overtures, and Caliban recognizes only that he has committed punishable offences, not that he has done wrong. In Caliban Shakespeare brings to life an image of nature from *King Lear*:

> *Allow not nature more than nature needs,*
> *Man's life is cheap as beast's.*

> (II.4.266)

These are Lear's words as he begs Goneril to understand, in his wish to retain his knights, the requirements of human dignity. But Goneril has no love or sympathy for her father, and does not hesitate to reduce him to the lowest level she can. Shakespeare provides one embodiment of man brought down to the condition of a beast in Poor Tom; Caliban is another version of this idea. Poor Tom is a social outcast, unprotected in a cruel and unproviding natural world and barely able to keep himself alive on the leavings of animals; by contrast Caliban lives in a world where nature is benevolent and he can enjoy what is freely available, but his own being is inherently bestial. Prospero calls him

> *A devil, a born devil, on whose nature*
> *Nurture can never stick;*

> (IV.1.188–9)

Caliban can rise above animal minimalism in one respect, through his sensual delight in the 'sounds and sweet airs' of the island, which bring him a vision of abundance:

> *... in dreaming,*
> *The clouds methought would open, and show riches*
> *Ready to drop upon me ...*

> (III.2.141–3)

Nature offers no such kind respite to Poor Tom. In both plays Shakespeare explores ideas about the natural world, placing his characters in a setting which calls into question assumptions about the values of society and civilization; he draws on the same polarities: the courtly and the natural, innocence and corruption, nature and nurture. Sebastian and Antonio have had the advantages of noble parentage and a court upbringing, but their failure to utilize their potential for spiritual improvement has made them liable to fall to a lower corruption even than Caliban. But Caliban, though natural, is not good; his instincts are for sex and power, and his contact with civilization in the shape of Trinculo and Stephano leads him only to abase and degrade himself. To a point he and Miranda have shared the same upbringing, as Prospero's pupils. Miranda has profited from Prospero's tutelage, but the inherent baseness of Caliban, his 'vile race' (I.2.358), is an immovable block to intellectual or spiritual advancement.

Though it will be hard to see any echoes of Lear and Cordelia in the relationship between Prospero and Miranda, Miranda is the last and perhaps the most shadowy of a line of regenerative daughter figures that begins with Cordelia and is carried on in Marina, Imogen and Perdita. In the other three romances, as in *King Lear*, the separation and reunion of father and daughter is an important motif; but in *The Tempest* Prospero is not a sinning or suffering father like Lear or Pericles or Leontes, so that the function of the young girl in restoring or forgiving her father at the climax of the play is not required. However, Miranda has acted as Prospero's preserver when her innocent hopefulness prevented him from despair during their dangerous sea-voyage:

> *O, a cherubim*
> *Thou wast that did preserve me. Thou didst smile,*
> *Infused with a fortitude from heaven,*
> *When I have decked the sea with drops full salt,*
> *Under my burden groaned, which rais'd in me*
> *An undergoing stomach, to bear up*
> *Against what should ensue.*

> (I.2.152–8)

Her angelic qualities are more lightly sketched in than Cordelia's or Marina's but her regenerative optimism and hope for the future, delicately expressed through her 'brave new world' exclamation at the sight of Alonso and the other courtiers, emerge triumphant at the play's conclusion, despite the muted response of Prospero to her enthusiasm: 'Tis new to thee'.

The Tempest gives final expression to a number of other favourite themes and motifs in Shakespeare, in particular the movement from false civilization to rugged but purgative nature culminating in the return to society, and the temporary absence or lapse of the ruler from power. As in many earlier plays Shakespeare explores the nature of power and authority, not only through ideas about secular rule in Prospero and Antonio, and the relationships between Naples and Milan, but also in a unique way, in the power Prospero exerts through Ariel. The process of discovering how *The Tempest* echoes Shakespeare's other plays is probably endless, but it is not futile. It reveals strikingly that although Shakespeare had his consistent preoccupations he never lost the ability to renew and transform them; and at the end of his theatrical career when his synthesizing powers were at their height, the creative force of his imagination had not deserted him.

The Jacobean context

The object of this section is to look at *The Tempest* in the context of its time, specifically the first decade of the seventeenth century, and to consider certain aspects of the current literary and theatrical scene which have particular bearing on the play, bringing out features of Shakespeare's dramaturgy which stand out in this context. I intend to isolate four topics: the theory of tragi-comedy, pastoral, the Jacobean masque, and Renaissance magic.

Tragi-comedy

It is generally accepted that Shakespeare's writing took a new direction after *Coriolanus* (1607/8) when he turned from tragedy to the mode of romantic tragi-comedy in *Pericles* and the other romances. Whether or not this was due to the influence of the Beaumont and Fletcher partnership, or more particularly to Fletcher, is a matter of dispute, but there is no doubt that changes in theatrical taste were taking place in the first decade of the seventeenth century, and that Shakespeare was responding to them. A significant indication of one kind of change is to be found in the 'Address to the Reader' written by Fletcher for his pastoral tragi-comedy *The Faithful Shepherdess*, a play of considerable interest for *The Tempest* despite its failure on stage. The play itself derives from the pastoral drama of the Italian writers Tasso and Guarini, whose poetic work was already known in England, and in his 'Address' Fletcher introduces the theoretical ideas of Guarini on the genre of tragi-comedy. The first critical pronouncement in English on the subject of tragi-comedy was by Sidney, who in his *Apologie for Poesie* (written in the 1580s but not published till 1595) had attacked it as a 'mongrel' form which attempted to combine the incompatible; Fletcher, however, following Guarini, defended and defined it as a new mode of drama emerging from the modifying of opposites:

> *A tragicomedy is not so called in respect of mirth and killing, but in respect it wants deaths, which is enough to make it no tragedy, yet brings some near it, which is enough to make it no comedy: which must be a representation of familiar people, with such kind of trouble as no life must be questioned; so*

that a God is as lawful in this as in a tragedy, and mean people as in a comedy.

(*The Faithful Shepherdess*, Address to the Reader, ?1609)

An extensive controversy over the aesthetic and moral validity of tragi-comedy had already been going on in Italy between Guarini and his opponent De Nores, a rigidly severe academic critic who disapproved of any departure from classical Aristotelian theory on the genres of drama, and, like Sidney, regarded tragi-comedy as an amalgam of the established modes of tragedy and comedy, which was unsatisfactory from all points of view. For the playwrights and theorists of this period, in England as well as on the Continent, the fact that, according to Aristotle and all his followers, tragedy dealt with noblemen and princes, and comedy with their social inferiors, was of the greatest importance. It imposed not only a social distinction between the styles of action and kinds of situation appropriate to each genre, but also a distinction of mood. Princes could not be made trivial or ridiculous, and peasants could not be ennobled. Hence the problem was not only one of justifying plots which began seriously but could be so worked out as to result in a happy ending, but also of providing a rationale and a dramatic technique for the mingling of moods. Guarini, who was the first critic to regard tragi-comedy as a species in its own right, describes how a tragicomic playwright selects elements from each genre so that they will interrelate and work to a single end:

[He] *takes from the one* [tragedy] *the great persons and not the actions, the fable verisimilar but not true, the affections moved but blunted, the delight but not the melancholy, the danger but not the death; from the other* [comedy], *the laughter that is not too relaxing, the modest amusements, the feigned complication, the happy reversal, and above all the comic order.*
(Quoted from M. Doran, *Endeavors of Art; A study of form in Elizabethan drama*, 1954, p. 207)

Though the theory of tragi-comedy was new in England at the beginning of the seventeenth century, the style of drama was not, and in fact the tragi-comedy of Beaumont and Fletcher may well have been the more acceptable because of its similarities with an earlier, native strain of writing in the popular romantic comedy. Plays such as *Mucedorus*, Green's *Friar Bacon and Friar Bungay*, Peele's *The Old Wives Tale* and Dekker's *Old Fortunatus* blended together pastoral elements, romantic adventures, knights and ladies, magic, myth and fairy-tale, and made up a represent-ative mode of English comedy. Though this sort of play went out of fashion for a little while, when the taste of the London theatre-goer after the turn of the century was more for satire and the Jonsonian social comedy of city life, there is a distinct sign of its return to favour in the revival by Shakespeare's company, the King's Men, of *Mucedorus* in 1610. *Mucedorus* (*c.* 1590) is a play with a princess lost in a wood, a prince disguised as a shepherd who loves her, a wild man, Bremo, who tries to capture her (and who may have influenced Shakespeare's Caliban), and a bear. If the number of printed editions is anything to go by, it was one of the most popular plays of its time, and in reviving it the King's Men must have been counting on a demand for the rambling drama of true, love and adventure in which all ends happily.

Thus Shakespeare's last plays appeared at a time when native tradition and continental theory came together in a mixed mode of drama. Though *Pericles* predates *The Faithful Shepherdess* and probably draws for its romantic elements on native tradition rather than on Guarini, *Cymbeline* and *The Winter's Tale* do seem to exhibit certain features of Guarini's dramaturgy, such as intricate plots with surprising discoveries, a mixture of high- and low-born characters, delayed revelations preceded by tension and suspense, and happy endings. *The Tempest*, because of its tauter time-scheme and more compact structure, is less dependent on elaborately contrived plotting and unexpected revelations, but even so it is distinctly a tragi-comedy, with characters from several strata of society, comic and serious styles of action, and several averted disasters. As late as the beginning of Act V there is still the chance of a serious ending, which, if not exactly 'unhappy' (since we should not expect Prospero to put any of his enemies to death despite their having intended to do so to him), would none the less not produce a final mood of reconciliation and harmony. Prospero is only persuaded to forgive his enemies by Ariel; this is so significant a point in the play that it is impossible to overemphasize it. As a result, Prospero is happily reconciled to his fellow-ruler, Alonso, King of Naples, and able to forgive the unresponsive Antonio; Stephano and Trinculo are duly humbled and Caliban penitent. All will return to Italy to celebrate Miranda and Ferdinand's wedding. The melancholy mood of the audience, aroused by the earlier action of the play, is purged in delight, according to Guarini's theory, and the workings of divine providence are demonstrated. 'Though the seas threaten, they are merciful', says Ferdinand.

Pastoral

The Italian play which had sparked off the controversy over tragi-comedy was Guarini's *Il Pastor Fido* (*The Faithful Shepherd*, published 1589), a tragi-comedy in a pastoral setting. The pastoral world provided an appropriate background for romantic adventure and was also unimpeachably classical in origin. English pastoral literature, like English tragi-comedy, represents a confluence of several currents of thought, not only the classical ideal, derived from Theocritus and Virgil, of the shepherd's life as an example of simple contentment and self-sufficiency, but also the Biblical concepts of the Good Shepherd and the shepherd-poet (in the Psalms of David, and the revival of classical pastoral centred on the idea of Arcadia as a country of the mind rather than of central Greece, celebrated in European pastoral poetry and romance such as the work of Tasso and Sannazaro in Italy, and Montemayor in Spain. In England literary pastoralism had been given a great impetus by Sidney's *Arcadia* in the 1580s and by parts of Spenser's *The Faerie Queene*. Shakespeare had drawn upon the mode and its conventions in his comedies, particularly *As You Like It*, which has for its source a pastoral prose romance, *Rosalynde*, by Thomas Lodge. Shakespeare, as always, transforms the conventions he adopts, through his dramatic genius for placing one set of attitudes within the perspective of another. Duke Senior expresses the typical feelings of a literary-minded Renaissance courtier towards country life:

> *Now, my co-mates and brothers in exile,*
> *Hath not old custom made this life more sweet*
> *Than that of painted pomp? Are not these woods*
> *More free from peril than the envious court?*

(II.1.1–2)

However, when the Duke proceeds to moralize away 'the penalty of Adam,/The seasons' difference', calling it one of the 'sweet' uses of adversity, this is less typical of the pastoral mode. In much non-Shakespearean pastoral poets revert to an ideal of the Golden Age where there is no change of season, spring is eternal, and the ease and contentment of country life are readily available to all who seek them. But in *As You Like It* the worlds of court and country are compared, and neither found to be absolutely desirable in itself: 'Good manners at the court are as ridiculous in the country as the behaviour of the country is most mockable at court!' (III.2.42). None the less the courtiers flock to the Forest of Arden to 'fleet the time carelessly as they did in the Golden World' and the pastoral sojourn has a universally beneficial effect, at least on those who intend to return to court in the end. In *King Lear* and *Timon of Athens* Shakespeare looks more equivocally at the courtier in the countryside, and depicts nature in much less rosy terms. Lear on the heath, though free from the cruel hypocrisy and deceptions of his daughters, is exposed to the harshness of elements which do not respect his age or status, just as Timon, having escaped the flatteries of 'trencher-friends, time's flies, cape-and-knee slaves' at court, finds himself bitterly digging for roots to eat in the woods. In the romances Shakespeare returns to a sunnier pastoral world, and explores again many of the familiar themes; in particular, he is concerned with the relationship between virtue and upbringing. Can country people, who have never known the life and standards of educated or courtly society, like the fishermen in *Pericles* or the shepherd and the clown in *The Winter's Tale*, be good? Can country life afford an appropriate arena for those with the finest moral sensibilities, like the two royal princes, Guiderius or Arviragus in *Cymbeline*, to realize themselves? Can exposure to the simple life of shepherds help to cure courtly vices or perfect the virtues of those of noble birth? Shakespeare's great contemporaries, Sidney and Spenser, also concerned themselves with those questions, and although they frequently depicted country people as both happy and virtuous in a pastoral setting, for knights and princesses and courtiers a return to the world of court was inevitable for true fulfilment. In the romances, where the central characters are all people of noble birth, the same is the case, and providence asserts itself so as to ensure that the courtiers who, for various reasons, have found themselves in an alien country environment, like Imogen in the Welsh hills or Prospero and Miranda on their island, are reinstated in their proper setting.

The Renaissance debate about pastoral life and values can be related to other current thinking on the whole subject of nature and cultivation, or nature and art. Montaigne in his essay 'Of the Cannibals', which, in Florio's translation of 1603, is an important source for *The Tempest* (see pp. 80–82), puts forward the proposition that man in his natural condition is happier and better off than in society, and that the Indians of North America embody an ideal primitivism:

> *For me seemeth that what in those nations* [the North American Indians] *we see by experience, doth not only exceed all the pictures wherewith licentious Poesie hath proudly imbellished the golden age, and all her quaint inventions to faine a happy condition of man, but also the conception and desire of Philosophie. They could not imagine a genuitie* [simplicity] *so pure and simple, as we see it by experience.*

Caliban, whose name is a near anagram of 'cannibal', is in part Shake-speare's contribution to this debate, though of course it is important to remember that his natural inclinations may be traced back to his semi-diabolic parentage; he is no islander 'pure and simple', but both cunning and corrupt. Gonzalo's vision of an ideal commonwealth, about which he fantasizes in an effort to divert Alonso (II.1.146–68) using phrases that echo Florio's Montaigne directly, is a poignant but essentially absurd version of the civilized man's longing for happy primitivism and pastoral contentment:

> All things in common nature should produce
> Without sweat or endeavour. Treason, felony,
> Sword, pike, knife, gun, or need of any engine
> Would I not have; but nature should bring forth
> Of its own kind all foison, all abundance,
> To feed my innocent people.

(II.1.163–8)

Much of the charm of pastoral derives from the ambivalence between the sophistication of its forms and styles, and the idea of simplicity which it celebrates. The poets of pastoral are not themselves primitive or simple and their work is highly artful, and conscious of its place in a long literary tradition.

The Jacobean masque

Another contemporary literary form which has significant bearing on *The Tempest* is the court masque. This form, though earlier versions of it had existed, developed during the reign of James I, whose wife, Queen Anne of Denmark, was an enthusiastic performer, as a splendid and expensive court entertainment which might be used for political ends. It was a short piece of dramatic allegory which provided opportunities for music, song and dance as well as the exchange of spoken dialogue, and in which lords and ladies of the court, even the monarch himself, might, without impropriety, take part along with professional performers. These enter-tainments were lavish and spectacular, in order both to display the power and prestige of the monarch and to compliment the invited guests, often visiting ambassadors from foreign countries. In the reigns of monarchs before James, the literary quality of these pieces was often negligible, though during the reign of Elizabeth the poetic possibilities of the genre became more evident, and it began to attract writers like George Gascoigne and George Peele, and in the seventeenth century Beaumont, Daniel,

Jonson and even Milton. None the less, the masque was essentially an occasional form, commissioned to suit specific circumstances and performed once or twice only. The chief participants were mostly not professional players, and their parts had to be devised accordingly, although performers in the anti-masque or 'antic masque', a comic or grotesque counter-action functioning as contrast to the masque proper, might be drawn from the professional companies.

It has been suggested that the structure of *The Tempest* as a whole is influenced by the masque, and hence that the play may really be seen as a vehicle for stage spectacle, song and dance with a light underlying moral meaning, rather than as a serious drama. This view is so (seriously) belittling to Shakespeare's play as to be untenable but it is clear that there are connections between the play and the masque. Enid Welsford, in her book *The Court Masque*, suggests that *The Tempest* may have been influenced by three particular masques of Jonson, *Hymenaei*, *The Masque of Blackness* and *The Masque of Beauty*, and that Shakespeare not only provided the dancing, music and spectacle to suit the tastes of an audience used to novelty and spectacle on stage, but also made use of masque conventions to express what she calls 'an intuition about life' (p. 347). The Caliban plot was perhaps a kind of Jonsonian anti-masque in the grotesquerie of its characters and action, dramatizing qualities deliberately antithetical to those in the main plot. Caliban, who is described by Stephano as 'some monster of the isle with four legs' is so strange in appearance that both Trinculo and Antonio think he could be exhibited as a freak at a fair; 'wild men' of various kinds had been popular in plays and pageants since the middle ages, and animal-headed creatures sometimes appeared in Tudor shows and Jacobean masques, like Comus' rabble in Milton's masque, symbolizing forces of disharmony and disorder. Ariel is another masque-like figure and there is a considerable amount of contemporary description and illustration of the stage costumes for elemental spirits and deities which suggests how he might have looked. Allardyce Nicoll's book, *Stuart Masques and the Renaissance Stage*, gives some examples. Ariel may owe something in conception and appearance to the musicians in *Hymenaei* who, 'figuring *airie* spirits, their habits various and resembling the several colours, caused in that part of the aire by reflexion' were seated within a rainbow and led by the famous musician Alphonso Ferrabosco. Prospero, who ends Caliban's misrule, functions rather like a masque presenter, in that he manipulates the actions of the human characters and his spirit-servants. He displays the spectacle for the benefit of the audience and in the epilogue steps forward as intermediary between his characters and the actors.

The themes of transformation and transience, so central to Shakespeare's play, are also basic to the whole nature of masque, where the materials of the scenic displays and the descriptions of the settings (especially Jonson's) stress both the insubstantiality of these beautiful devices, and also their capacity for sudden and total change into something quite different. In a general way, Prospero's speech to Ferdinand and Miranda, after he has broken off the betrothal-masque, uses theatrical imagery to express the idea of the beauty and transience of life, but there may be more specific connections with masque: in mood it resembles a passage from *Hymenaei*, where the author laments the briefness of the spectacle's glory:

> *Such was the exquisit performance, as* (*beside the* pompe, splendor, *or what we may call* apparelling *of such* Presentments) *that alone* (*had all else beene absent*) *was of power to surprise with delight, and steale away the* spectators *from themselues. Nor was there wanting whatsoeuer might give to the* furniture, *or* complement; *eyther in* riches, *or the strangenesse of the* habites, *delicacie of* daunces, *magnificence of the* scene, *or diuine rapture of* musique. *Onely the enuie was, that it lasted not still, or* (*now it is past*) *cannot by imagination, much lesse description, be recovered to a part of that* spirit *it had in the gliding by.*

(Jonson, Works, ed. Herford and Simpson, VII, 229)

Ferdinand is moved with delight at Prospero's show, just as Alonso and the other courtiers are in Act III, Scene 3, when they are presented with Prospero's banquet of spirits, and in each scene there is that blend of the rich, delicate and strange which Jonson mentions, a majestic vision all the more potent and enchanting for its extreme ephemerality. In the speech at Act IV, Scene 1, the words 'revels', 'pageant' and 'rack' are all semi-technical terms with specific meanings in the context of masque (although of course they have other general meanings too), and 'rack' in particular was used of stage clouds which could be made to appear to dissolve, and so in the absence of a curtain or a black-out, end one scene of action and provide a moment of transition to the next. It is tempting to imagine that the 'cloud-capp'd towers, the gorgeous palaces' of Prospero's speech would have had an extra significance for those members of his audience privileged to view the expensively insubstantial pageantry of the masque at court.

Renaissance magic

The masque expresses one form of the Jacobean fascination with mysterious appearances, transient manifestations, and the spirit world. Another form is seen by contemporary theories and practices of magic. That Shakespeare was profoundly interested in the supernatural is evident in many ways from plays as different as *A Midsummer Night's Dream*, *Hamlet* and *Macbeth*; he was familiar with different aspects of it, perhaps from special study (as we see for instance from the theories of demonology in *Hamlet*, and the practice of witchcraft in *Macbeth*). In *The Tempest*, however, he is concerned with elemental magic, and in Prospero he shows us an example of the magus, or white witch, the adept who has attained the highest levels of his art and discovered the power to command spirits and even to control nature.

Prospero is no conjurer or wizard, dressing up in magic robes and waving a wand to perform spells or charms; and he has nothing in common with the witches in *Macbeth* whose methods are those of the contemporary witch or wise woman, as documented in accounts of current witch trials. Shakespeare clearly differentiates him both from this semi-respectable world of folk-magic and also from the unorthodox traffic with necromancy of Marlowe's *Dr Faustus*. His closest Shakespearean parallel is Oberon in *A Midsummer Night's Dream*, but Prospero is a human not a supernatural being, who has built up his magic powers over a long period of time and study. He is a learned man and a scholar who has turned his scholarship to a particular direction – the study of magical arts. It would be inappropriate to call this 'natural' magic, although it gives Prospero control over the natural world, since 'natural' magic is the lowest form of magic, and Prospero has superseded it. According to the *De Occulta Philosophia* (1533) of Cornelius Agrippa ('the handbook of Renaissance occult sciences', as Frances Yates in *The Occult Philosophy in the Elizabethan Age*, 1979, p. 40, calls it), supernatural power can be subdivided into three: the natural or elemental, the celestial (which relates to stars and planets), and the supercelestial or intellectual (which concerns the control of spirits and intelligences); Prospero's arts give him control in each of these spheres. It is important to realize that for people of Shakespeare's time there were not the same distinctions between religion, philosophy and magic as now; the rediscovery of Plato's dialogues in the Renaissance, and the translation of them into Latin by the Florentine scholar Marsilio Ficino in the fifteenth century, encouraged the idea of the philosopher Plato as a proponent of an ancient system of magic, and led to the association of his writings with those of the mystical Hermes Trismegistus, then supposed (wrongly) to be a contemporary of Moses and prophet of Christianity.

Ficino's book *De Vita Coelitus Comparanda* (1489) deals with the relationship between astral or planetary influences and human life through the medium of a cosmic spirit, and especially with methods of attracting planetary influences. Agrippa's *De Occulta Philosophia* develops Ficino's ideas, bringing in a system of mathematical (or numerological) magic derived from Pythagoras, and dealing more boldly than did Ficino with the implications of the magical requirement for spirits or demonic forces to act as agents for the power passing between the planets and man. In the England of Elizabeth I the magical practitioner and alchemist John Dee who followed the doctrines of Agrippa and of the German alchemist Paracelsus was, for his time, an important figure, if always equivocal. His fine library of works in magic and demonology was consulted by Sir Philip Sidney and a whole circle of learned men including the mathematician Sir Thomas Allen, and explorer Martin Frobisher, though he was isolated and disgraced in his later years.

Mystical ideas about the ways in which man might learn through the exercise of a refined and disciplined spiritual will to harness planetary forces and thereby exercise influence over the natural world, also to be found in the writings of Plato's Christian followers Plotinus and Porphyry, were deeply stimulating and provocative to the thinkers of this period but not always easy to distinguish from systems of demonic thought. The magic of Ficino and Agrippa was condemned on religious grounds by many; distrust of astrology and by implication the whole way of thinking that was based on belief in a system of inherent correspondences linking all the component elements of the created universe, from stones up to angelic beings, is encapsulated in Jonson's play *The Alchemist*, which is almost contemporary with *The Tempest*. A comparison between the two plays makes it clear that, even if Prospero cannot necessarily be regarded as a sympathetic portrait of Dr Dee, as Yates suggests, Shakespeare's play does show magic being practised by a wise and learned man for good ends. Various details define Prospero as the scholar-magician. He tells Miranda that his life on the desolate island has been made bearable by the forethought of Gonzalo, who provided him 'with volumes that I prize above my dukedom' as well as more utilitarian items, so that he has been enabled to pursue the scholarship in which he was already deeply involved before his expulsion from Milan. He is seen to repair to his studies at the end of Act III, Scene 1, not simply for abstract pleasure but, apparently, for practical instruction:

> *I'll to my book,*
> *For yet ere suppertime must I perform*
> *Much business ...* (III.1.94–6)

Caliban refers several times to his master's books, which he regards superstitiously as the source of Prospero's power:

> *... thou mayst brain him,*
> *Having first seized his books ... Remember*
> *First to possess his books, for without them*
> *He's but a sot, as I am, nor hath not*
> *One spirit to command. They all do hate him*
> *As rootedly as I. Burn but his books.*

> (III.2.89–93)

Perhaps he is not entirely wrong, for when Prospero prepares in the last act to give up his magic for good, he intends not simply to abandon his book but to drown it 'deeper than did ever plummet sound'. The intensity of the feeling here perhaps implies that the book must be prevented from getting into the wrong hands at all costs.

With the aid of his book, and also, it seems, of the special properties of his staff and his robe, Prospero can control both the natural and the supernatural world. Ariel is the medium through which his commands are carried out, and below Ariel are apparently infinite numbers of subsidiary spirits. Prospero's powers are awe-inspiring:

> *... to the dread rattling thunder*
> *Have I given fire, and rifted Jove's stout oak*
> *With his own bolt; the strong-based promontory*
> *Have I made shake, and by the spurs plucked up*
> *The pine and cedar; graves at my command*
> *Have waked their sleepers, oped, and let 'em forth*
> *By my so potent art.*

> (V.1.44–50)

'Art' is the word he regularly uses for his magical skills, thereby distinguishing them from those of the play's other magician, Sycorax, who seems to have been introduced for the purpose of contrasting with Prospero. She too had fearsome powers over the natural world, but directed to low and malignant ends, and more limited than Prospero's; she had imprisoned Ariel within the trunk of a pine tree, but she had not the skill to release him. Caliban, her son, compares Sycorax with Prospero, and resentfully recognizes the superior skills of his master:

> *I must obey. His art is of such power,*
> *It would control my dam's god Setebos,*
> *And make a vassal of him.*

> (I.2.372–4)

Sycorax, though by implication a 'New World' witch with special affinities

35

with the natural resources of the island, some of which Caliban inherits, actually comes from the Old World, from Algiers, from where she was banished for practising 'sorceries terrible to enter human hearing'; and she has some of the qualities of classical witches such as Medea and Circe. The natural powers through which Sycorax can operate by means of her charms and cursing are low ones; she has no access to the higher spiritual magic available to Prospero through his learning and refinement of mind. Technically, they are contrasted as practitioners of 'goety' and 'theurgy', to use the terminology of Agrippa (*Of the Vanity of Artes and Sciences*, translated by J. Sanford 1569), one the necromancer who traffics with evil spirits and the other the holy magician who works through good spirits and angelic powers.

There is clear evidence in *The Tempest* of a background of technical knowledge and of specific systems of Renaissance magic, and there is no doubt that many references to the spiritual world which are vague or figurative to us would have had precise meanings for Shakespeare's audience. But it is equally important that such elements in the play, which originate from its Jacobean context, can still be perceived as part of the play's total meaning, vitally contributing to, and enriching, its significance.

Structure and imagery

The Tempest is Shakespeare's second shortest play, so short, in fact, that it has sometimes been thought to be an abridgement of a longer version, now lost. Even so, it is a play with a good deal of action. Romance as a mode, like tragi-comedy, puts a strong stress on plenty of things happening; in *The Tempest* all the major and most of the minor characters experience a change of fortune, and there are several separate lines of action. But it is important to be aware that the patterning or design of events can be as significant in contributing to the overall aesthetic effect and to the meaning as the events themselves. The fact that all the action takes place within a few hours plays a large part in determining the arrangement of these events. The observation of the unity of time, something Shakespeare had hitherto shown little concern for, is matched by that of unity of place, and, in a sense, unity of action. The resultant compression and close interrelationship of all the parts of the play is not common to the romance; the rambling quality and loose structures of *Pericles* or *The Winter's Tale*, with the action taking place over a number of years and in several locations, are much more typical.

Near the beginning of the play Prospero asks Ariel the time and emphasizes that much has to be accomplished in a few hours: 'The time 'twixt six and now/Must by us both be spent most preciously' (I.2.240–41). In the last scene a comment of the Boatswain's draws attention to the speed with which everything has happened:

> *. . . our ship –*
> *Which, but three glasses since, we gave out split –*
> *Is light and yare and bravely rigged, as when*
> *We first put out to sea.*

(V.1.222–5)

The effect of speed, and also of careful planning on the part of Prospero, is achieved not only by these references, but also by the interlocking of the play's various strands of action. Though it is possible to discern quite clearly the outlines of different elements that combine together to compose this play, what is really striking is the close interrelation of the parts.

A five-act structure, conforming to the academic theories advocated by neo-classical critics of the Renaissance who followed the example of Plautus and Terence, forms the basis for the play, with a prologue in the shipwreck scene, *protasis* or exposition in Act I where all but two of the characters (Stephano and Trinculo) are presented, complications introduced in Act II, complications intensified (*epitasis*) in Act III, coming to crisis point in Act IV, with *catastrophe* or resolution in Act V. Moving concurrently through those various stages of development are three separate plot-lines involving separate groups of characters: the courtiers, their villainy and their punishment; the disorderly desires of Caliban, Stephano and Trinculo; and the courtship and betrothal of Ferdinand and Miranda. These are subsumed under the general action of Prospero's plan for revenging himself on his enemies and resuming his role as Duke of Milan. The various plot-lines are set in motion by a single event, the shipwreck, which brings Prospero's enemies to his island and introduces Caliban and Miranda to the first human beings other than Prospero they have ever seen. Because Shakespeare has chosen to limit the time-span of stage-action so drastically, considerable exposition is needed to provide a context for the present situation, so Prospero must tell Miranda, as early as possible, his reasons for causing the shipwreck, and with them the reasons why they are living as they are on the island. Once Prospero, his daughter, and also his two contrasting servants, Ariel and Caliban, have been established, each action is then separately introduced. In Act I, Scene 2, the newly landed Ferdinand, lured by Ariel's music, catches sight of Miranda. This takes us a little by surprise, since although the imminent appearance of a number of characters from Prospero's past has been prepared for, Ferdinand is not one of them. The action, then, will not consist entirely of retribution for past events, but will also contain elements directed towards the future, and the two young people instantly fall in love, as Prospero observes.

In Act II, Scene 1, the courtiers who have already been introduced to us in Prospero's exposition come on, chief among them Ferdinand's father, Alonso, mourning the loss of the son he believes drowned, and Prospero's wicked brother, Antonio. Antonio's project of murdering Alonso and with him Gonzalo, so that Sebastian may seize the throne of Naples as Antonio has that of Milan, is foiled by Ariel's music. In Act II, Scene 2, Caliban meets Stephano and Trinculo who believe the courtiers to be drowned and who plan, with Caliban's assistance, to take over the rule of the island. In Act III each action is separately developed, and the courtiers' plot brought to a climax when Ariel appears to them as a harpy and denounces the 'three men of sin', showing them how their present predicament is a punishment for their crime against Prospero:

> *. . . remember –*
> *For that's my business to you – that you three*
> *From Milan did supplant good Prospero,*
> *Exposed unto the sea, which hath requit it,*
> *Him and his innocent child; for which foul deed*
> *The powers, delaying, not forgetting, have*
> *Incensed the seas and shores, yea, all the creatures*
> *Against your peace.*

> (III.3.69–76)

In different ways, each man is deeply affected by Ariel's speech. 'All three of them are desperate', comments Gonzalo as they rush from the stage in passion:

> *Their great guilt,*
> *Like poison given to work a great time after,*
> *Now 'gins to bite the spirits.*

> (III.3.106–8)

In Act IV, in a single scene of fluid action, the other two plots also reach the end of their development. Prospero celebrates the betrothal of Ferdinand and Miranda (which has all along been his real object, despite his apparent hostility towards it earlier) with a masque of spirits, but breaks off in a sudden perturbation at the recollection of Caliban's plot against him which must be foiled at once. The scene ends with Ariel distracting Stephano and Trinculo from the project and then punishing all three. At the beginning of Act V Prospero makes the point that all is now prepared for the denouement, or, in classical terms, the catastrophe – here, of course, a comic (or happy) one.

PROSPERO: *Now does my project gather to a head.*
             My charms crack not, my spirits obey, and time
             Goes upright with his carriage. How's the day?
ARIEL: *On the sixth hour, at which time, my lord*
             You said our work should cease.
PROSPERO: *I did say so,*
             When first I raised the tempest.

> (V.1.1–6)

The extraordinary neatness and compression of the structure is underlined. Prospero, like Shakespeare, is proud of his skill as a planner. One thing only must take place before the whole company can be assembled for the reunion: Prospero's extraordinary change of heart. This is the crucial change in a play about metamorphosis. Up to this point – and with the exception of his plans for Ferdinand and Miranda – Prospero's interests have been energetically directed to revenge. Now, prompted by Ariel – a supernatural figure not compelled by human feelings – he is forced to recognize his own humanity, to forgive his enemies and to realize that 'the rarer action is/In virtue than in vengeance', and that since his enemies are penitent, nothing remains to be accomplished: 'The sole drift of my purpose doth extend/Not a frown further' (V.1.29–30).

Each group in turn comes before him starting with the courtiers, Alonso ready at once to relinquish the usurped throne, but Antonio ambiguously silent. The 'discovery' of Ferdinand and Miranda playing chess convinces Gonzalo, always optimistic, that things have truly turned out for the best. The Boatswain and Master appear next to tell the court (and the audience) of the miraculous preservation of their vessel. Finally Ariel drives in Caliban, Stephano and Trinculo, chastened and abashed before an audience of their betters, and the servants, their social aspirations abandoned, revert to their proper status. Prospero and the rest prepare to return to Naples on the morrow while Ariel, at last, takes his freedom.

Within this neatly planned structure Shakespeare creates pattern and design by means of parallels and contrasts. Relationships and situations are duplicated or echoed; events in one plot repeat or parody those in another. As Prospero has in the past been supplanted by his brother, Antonio, so Antonio on the island urges Sebastian to supplant his brother, Alonso. Sebastian is persuaded to attempt a second act of usurpation, not realizing that Antonio's original unbrotherly act is the cause of their present predicament:

> *Thy case, dear friend,*
> *Shall be my precedent. As thou got'st Milan*
> *I'll come by Naples.*

(II.1.295–7)

A second murder attempt is planned by Stephano, Trinculo and Caliban. Stephano, set on by his lust for Miranda and by Caliban's desire for vengeance on his master, decides to kill Prospero and take over the island. For the bestial Caliban, the drunken butler with his 'celestial liquor' seems like a 'brave god' with powers more deserving of worship than Prospero's, and Caliban seeks to replace one master with another. In both cases Ariel is at hand with his music to foil the projects. Brother turns against brother, and servant against master. Patterning takes other forms of duplication and of contrast. Prospero and Alonso are two fathers initially enemies, whose children fall in love. Prospero's greatest enemy is his brother, Antonio, whose usurpation has been followed by an attempt at murder, and in their relationship can be seen that archetypal pairing of good and bad siblings that Shakespeare is so fond of (consider Don Pedro and Don John in *Much Ado About Nothing*, Orlando and Oliver in *As You Like It*, old Hamlet and Claudius in *Hamlet*). Sebastian also tries to usurp his brother's place and kill him.

The good and the evil are again compared in Prospero and the island's other ruler, the witch Sycorax, as proponents respectively of white and of black magic: where Sycorax imprisoned Ariel in a tree-trunk because he was a spirit 'too delicate to act her earthy and abhorred commands', Prospero has released him and recognized the full potentialities of his 'dainty' servant's nature. Even the offspring of Prospero and Sycorax are morally contrasted, the innocent Miranda and the ignorant Caliban, who are alike in knowing nothing of life in society but dissimilar in their responses to education; for the naturally teachable Miranda Prospero has been an effective schoolmaster and

> ... *made thee more profit*
> *Than other princess can, that have more time*
> *For vainer hours, and tutors not so careful.*

> (I.2.172–4)

Caliban is another matter, 'a devil, a born devil, on whose nature/Nurture can never stick'. Caliban's nature is that of a slave and an underling. Although he hates the toil he must do for Prospero his immediate instinct is to grovel and cower when faced with Stephano: 'I'll kiss thy foot; I'll swear myself thy subject'. Like Ferdinand he is a would-be suitor to Miranda. In this role Ferdinand is a willing servant and, though a prince, yet his mistress's 'patient log-man', while Caliban is without graces and conscious only of lust, having, as Prospero has already told us, attempted to rape Miranda.

Even the lovers themselves are contrasted: the sophisticated Ferdinand, who has 'ey'd with best regard ... full many a lady' and often fallen in love before, and Miranda who has seen only one man in her life. Caliban as servant is contrasted, of course, with Ariel, the gross and the spiritual, earth and air. The one plots with enemies against his master, while the other assists his master's projects for retribution and is himself the agent of the final reconciliation. In Caliban is all the brutishness and disorder of unregenerate nature, while Ariel foils plots, prevents murders, brings lovers together, and with his music works for peace and harmony.

The Tempest is a very highly-wrought play, densely patterned and intricate in design. The replication of motifs in its structure allows for a certain sort of dramatic shorthand, by which characters or actions are defined in relation to each other and to their function in the story, and not developed or elaborated in their own right. Hence Miranda and Ferdinand are young lovers, both noble of birth and dutiful as children, but completely opposite in upbringing and experience. Some aspects of each character are further defined in relation to Caliban (Miranda's innocence and natural refinements, Ferdinand's sophisticated sexuality). Shakespeare does not, for the purposes of his play, need to explore their situation any further. Antonio is the wicked brother unrepentant, whose natural malignity leads him to corrupt another into a repetition of his own crime; the extent of his evil may be measured against that of Stephano, a 'low' character and a servant, who has not Antonio's advantages of birth and therefore possibly has more motivation for his criminal envy of Prospero.

The language in the play shares the qualities of compression and density to be found in the structure. *The Tempest* by its nature is a play with a great deal of narration, which needs to be concise and vivid if it is not to slow up the action. In addition to Prospero's account to Miranda of his past misfortunes and his brother's treachery, Ariel has to tell Prospero how he has 'perform'd' the tempest, and also at a later point how he has lured Caliban and his companions into a filthy pond by playing his pipe. Francisco describes Ferdinand's attempt to escape drowning, and the Boatswain relates, as best he can, his strange experience of surviving the tempest and rejoining the passengers of his ship on the island. All of these passages are notable for their compression, and some of them for the liveliness of their language. Each narrator has a different manner of speech and his own linguistic individuality – even the Boatswain, who is given hardly thirty lines in the whole play. Not only has Prospero a complicated tale to tell Miranda, but he must tell it in such a way as to express his own strong feelings about the past. Shakespeare gives him a fast-moving style rich in metaphor and suggestive of urgency by the way in which words are omitted and the syntax compressed:

> *Thy false uncle . . .*
> *Being once perfected how to grant suits,*
> *How to deny them, who t'advance, and who*
> *To trash for over-topping, new created*
> *The creatures that were mine, I say, or changed 'em,*
> *Or else new formed 'em; having both the key*
> *Of officer and office, set all hearts i'th'state*
> *To what tune pleased his ear, that now he was*

> *The ivy which had hid my princely trunk,*
> *And sucked my verdure out on't.*

> (I.2.77–87)

'Perfected' should probably be followed by 'in knowing' to be more correct, but the meaning is clear and the effect more forceful without these words; 'to trash for over-topping' means to hold back from exceeding authority, using a metaphor from hunting in 'trash', and achieving vividness through the alliteration; the interjection 'I say' gives a colloquial effect and implies the speaker's emotion at this point; the idea of the 'key' of the office leads into the musical image 'set ... to what tune pleased his ear' and economically expresses the idea of Antonio's complete takeover of power with suggestions of tyranny and total authority; the last metaphor, of Antonio overwhelming Prospero like ivy growing over a tree, implies the poisonous and parasitical nature of Antonio's power; the omission of 'and' before 'having' (l. 83) and 'so' before 'that' (l. 85) speeds up Prospero's flow and makes his rhythm more abrupt.

Ariel's account of his part in the tempest, which follows soon after, is done in quite a different style.

> *I boarded the King's ship. Now on the beak,*
> *Now in the waist, the deck, in every cabin*
> *I flamed amazement. Sometime I'd divide,*
> *And burn in many places. On the topmast,*
> *The yards, and boresprit would I flame distinctly,*
> *Then meet and join. Jove's lightnings, the precursors*
> *O'th' dreadful thunderclaps, more momentary*
> *And sight-outrunning were not. The fire and cracks*
> *Of sulphurous roaring the most mighty Neptune*
> *Seems to besiege, and make his bold waves tremble,*
> *Yea, his dread trident shake.*

> (I.2.196–206)

This speech stresses speed of movement, vividness, supernatural power. The parts of the ship are enumerated – 'beak ... waist ... deck ...' – and Ariel's rapid transitions between them detailed; his body behaves like something inhuman (which it is), and his activities are described in verbs not normally used of human motion – 'I flamed', 'I'd divide, and burn', 'meet and join'. Syntax is again compressed: 'I flamed amazement' must mean something like 'I caused terror by bursting into flames'. The unexpected word-order and irregular rhythms of 'Jove's lightnings ... were not' convey Ariel's excitement at the memory, and perhaps imitate the quality of his movement.

Techniques such as compression of syntax, omission of connective words, alteration of word-order, and irregularity of rhythm characterize much of the language of this play, and indeed are well-known features of Shakespeare's later blank verse. They are found in many of the more memorable passages of *The Tempest*, for instance in Caliban's 'Be not afeared; the isle is full of noises', where the mingling of different verb tenses and the extra syllables at the ends of some lines help to create the effects of enchantment and of dream in Caliban's experience. In Ferdinand's memorable lines,

> *... Sitting on a bank,*
> *Weeping again the King my father's wrack,*
> *This music crept by me upon the waters,*
> *Allaying both their fury and my passion*
> *With its sweet air ...*

> (I.2.390–94)

Shakespeare again achieves something of the quality of memory and hallucination by giving Ferdinand participles ('sitting ... weeping') without an expressed subject, as well as by his use of alliteration on 'w', and extra syllables at the ends of the lines (in 'waters' and 'passion'). But Shakespeare does not necessarily have to experiment with the rules of grammar and meter to achieve compression; he can do it with the simplest of diction and syntax:

> *'Tis as impossible that he's undrowned*
> *As he that sleeps here swims.*

> (II.1.241–2)

> *Here lies your brother,*
> *No better than the earth he lies upon,*
> *If he were that which now he's like – that's dead –*

> (II.1.285–7)

The lines are spoken by Antonio, a man whose curt style of speech fits his business-like way of dealing with moral issues:

> *Twenty consciences*
> *That stand 'twixt me and Milan, candied be they,*
> *And melt ere they molest.*

> (II.1.283–5)

His figurative language is appropriate to his manner; he uses more metaphors and similes than most characters in this play, and always vivid ones of immediate appeal, never developed at length; to him Gonzalo is an 'ancient morsel' and the other courtiers easily manipulated: 'They'll take suggestion as a cat laps milk'. His conscience is less trouble to him than a chilblain: 'if 'twere a kibe,/'twould put me to my slipper'.

The play is, perhaps unexpectedly, not rich in figurative language. Wilson Knight in *The Crown of Life* suggests that this is because it 'is itself metaphor' (p. 224) and because several of Shakespeare's favourite sources of imagery, such as storms, the sea, music, animal sounds and other natural objects, occur anyway as part of the action of the play. By saying that the play is a metaphor Wilson Knight perhaps means that all of the events in it may be taken to stand, both individually and in their relationships to each other, for something else; but they are in themselves poetic events, and work on our imagination as the words and images in a poem. Ariel turning into a flame to astonish the mariners in the storm or denouncing the 'three men of sin', Caliban cursing Prospero and describing the effects of Prospero's curses on him, Prospero bidding farewell to his 'rough magic' – all of these passages relate to events astonishing and suggestive enough in themselves to stimulate the imagination without the need for the intensification of metaphorical language. Here, in fact, imagery might even distract from the clarity and directness of Shakespeare's vision. The three songs of Ariel are among the most beautiful Shakespeare ever wrote, but their quality derives from sources other than metaphorical language; they epitomize both the rich sense of the natural world that pervades the play and also its potentiality for transformation into the world of the supernatural.

The multifarious forms of nature are vividly present in the play's language; in the tasks Ariel performs for Prospero, rising at midnight 'to fetch dew/From the still-vexed Bermoothes', commanded

> ... *to tread the ooze*
> *Of the salt deep,*
> *To run upon the sharp wind of the north,*
> *To do me business in the veins o'th' earth*
> *When it is baked with frost* ...

(I.2.252–6)

in the curses of Caliban and Prospero, and in the accounts of the varied resources of the island. We hear of the 'fresh-brook mussels, wither'd roots, and husks/Wherein the acorn cradled' that Ferdinand will be condemned to eat, the 'pig-nuts', 'clustering filberts' and 'young scamels from the rock' that Caliban offers to Stephano, the lush green grass that Gonzalo perceives around him, the 'toothed briars, sharp furzes, pricking goss, and thorns' and the 'filthy-mantled pool' into which Ariel lures Stephano and his followers.

Nature is often referred to by characters who, unlike Prospero, are not adepts in magic (see pp. 32–6), in terms that imply a pervasively animistic spirit; the natural world is thought of as operating in a manner analogous to the behaviour of human beings, and sometimes as acting in response to them. Miranda's first speech describing the storm shows this conception of nature:

> *The sky it seems would pour down stinking pitch,*
> *But that the sea, mounting to th' welkin's cheek,*
> *Dashes the fire out.*

(I.2.3–5)

As is typical in this play, the implication of personification behind 'cheek' is not followed through, but sky and sea combat one another like opponents in a battle. Even Prospero, the magus, describing the exposure which he and Miranda underwent at sea, imagines nature with human attributes:

> *There they hoist us,*
> *To cry to th'sea that roared to us, to sigh*
> *To th' winds, whose pity sighing back again*
> *Did us but loving wrong.*

(I.2.148–51)

The idea of nature acting not only in a human way but also in harmony with human feeling is expressed in a number of phrases spoken by different characters throughout the play, from Caliban's curse on Prospero, 'All the infections that the sun sucks up ... on Prosper fall' (II.2.1) to Ariel's description of the 'toothed briars, sharp furzes, pricking goss, and thorns' (IV.1.180) which so actively torment Caliban and his drunken companions. The most important references to this idea come in Act III, Scene 3, when Ariel appears to Alonso and the courtiers in his harpy disguise and denounces them as 'men of sin'. Their offences against Prospero have aroused the anger of the whole natural world:

> *... The powers, delaying, not forgetting, have*
> *Incensed the seas and shores, yea, all the creatures*
> *Against your peace.*

(III.3.74–6)

Alonso immediately recognizes in the events of the storm and shipwreck nature's message of outrage:

> *O, it is monstrous, monstrous!*
> *Methought the billows spoke, and told me of it;*
> *The winds did sing it to me; and the thunder,*
> *That deep and dreadful organ-pipe, pronounced*
> *The name of Prosper: it did bass my trespass.*

(III.3.97–101)

Here the sound imagery Alonso uses builds to a climax, from the speech of the billows and the singing of the winds to the ground bass of the thunder: nature joins in musical harmony to accuse Alonso.

The single speech relying most heavily on figurative language is Prospero's famous 'Our revels now are ended'. It starts off from literal reality – the harvest dance of nymphs and shepherds devised for Ferdinand and Miranda's entertainment has been brought to a sudden end by Prospero's recollection of Caliban's conspiracy. The immediate and complete disappearance of the whole company of spirit actors naturally leads Prospero to philosophize on the similarity between this dissolving pageant, dreams and human life. Theatre and theatrical ideas underlie much of the play's action, and create a pattern of imagery: Ariel 'performs' the tempest, which Prospero refers to as a spectacle, and puts on several other shows at Prospero's bidding, for which he is praised:

> *Bravely the figure of this harpy hast thou*
> *Performed, my Ariel*

(III.3.84–5)

> *Thou and thy meaner fellows your last service*
> *Did worthily perform, and I must use you*
> *In such another trick. Go bring the rabble ...*

(IV.1.35–7)

Prospero envisages Antonio assuming the role of authority like an actor, and wanting 'no screen between this part he played/And him he played it for'. Antonio too uses theatrical language to Sebastian when hinting at Alonso's murder; he talks of the return journey from Claribel's wedding in Tunis as the potential setting for a decisive act. Claribel is

> *She that from whom*
> *We all were sea-swallowed, though some cast again,*
> *And, by that destiny, to perform an act*
> *Whereof what's past is prologue, what to come,*
> *In yours and my discharge.*

(II.1.254–8)

'Cast' initially means 'cast up', but is subsumed into a theatrical metaphor along with 'perform', 'act', 'prologue' and 'discharge', whereby life is compared with the acting out of a play. Prospero's speech does not take up Antonio's notion of determinism, but restricts the comparison between life and theatre to the idea of the transience of beauty and spectacle. Life is as short and insignificant as a play, or, in an extension of the comparison, a dream, and leaves as little trace behind. The elegiac tone and beauty of the phrasing have made the speech memorable; but, as with most of the imagery in *The Tempest*, its meaning comes largely from its particular context, rather than from association with a chain or series of similar images. None the less the language of the play is often powerfully vivid; and in its compression and inventiveness we see Shakespeare's mature art at its best.

Characters and themes

The Tempest is so peculiarly closely wrought and unified a play that it is more difficult, and perhaps more misleading, with this than with any other of Shakespeare's plays to extract one or other strand of meaning and separate it from the totality of the play for special attention. In attempting to do this one very quickly realizes how interdependent all the aspects of the play are, and how each derives its significance from its different relationships with all the rest. It is true that the characters divide readily into clear-cut groups: Prospero; Ariel and the spirit world; the young lovers Ferdinand and Miranda; Caliban, Stephano and Trinculo; the court party; the Boatswain and mariners. But even here there are possible cross-divisions and re-arrangements on other bases: Caliban, for instance, can belong with Ariel as Prospero's fellow-servant, though utterly antithetical in nature, or even with Miranda, as Prospero's protegé and a being who has grown up on the island without the advantages of society; and the court party may be subdivided, with Antonio and Sebastian, each a 'wicked brother', as a separate unit. Prospero, however, always stands apart, in isolation, his separateness a significant aspect of his being in several ways, so that he makes a natural starting-place for an exploration of the play's themes.

Prospero is a ruler and *The Tempest* is a study in power: spiritual and temporal; natural and supernatural; power over the outer world and power over the self. Though Shakespeare chooses to dramatize only four hours of Prospero's life, his past career is an important part of his present situation. Twelve years earlier he had been an important prince, ruler of the city-state of Milan, which he calls 'the first of all the signories' in Italy, but he was deposed by his brother Antonio who seized his throne and thrust him into exile. While Shakespeare was not attempting to relate this story to actual events in the history of Renaissance Italy, the general picture of turbulence and uneasy power-struggles between rival rulers is a reflection of how Jacobeans were encouraged by recent chroniclers to view Italian politics. Prospero in recounting his past to Miranda now accepts his own responsibility for the deposition; he has been naive in his understanding both of the duties of a ruler and of his brother's character, and thus incompetent as a prince. He has been too much concerned with the contemplative, and too little with the active life, 'neglecting worldly ends, all dedicated to closeness and the bettering of my mind'; in a

49

private individual such single-minded devotion to scholarship might be praiseworthy, but in a ruler it is dangerous, and leads directly to a coup d'état by Prospero's evil brother in collaboration with another power-seeking ruler, Alonso, King of Naples. It is important to recognize that although the glimpses of the world of power-politics in Italy that we are given in the recollections of Prospero, and the behaviour of Antonio or Sebastian on the island, are unappealing, this is the realism of activity to which Prospero wishes to return. 'Bountiful Fortune' has brought his enemies within his reach, and his magic powers have enabled him to make the most of the opportunity offered for retribution. It is a chance to restore his fallen fortunes, which he seizes, appearing to the amazed courtiers in Act V in his former guise as Duke of Milan, and demanding back his rights. The change of clothes he makes at Act V, Scene 1, line 58 is symbolic, as are clothing references throughout the play, of Prospero's identity, and can be related to the idea of change.

When we first see Prospero he is dressed as a magician, still in the garb in which he raised the storm; after a few moments he asks Miranda to 'pluck my magic garment from me' so that he may speak simply, as a father, but he probably resumes it later in the scene to encounter Ariel, and wears it for most of his other appearances (except when he is 'invisible', according to the stage direction, in Act III, Scene 3, line 18, where he wears a conventional stage gown to designate this condition). But in Act V he appears 'in his magic robes' to perform for the last time as a magician, and changes from these into his princely attire with Ariel's help, on stage and in full view of the courtiers who are at this point slowly emerging from the tranced condition into which Prospero has put them. The change of costume, carried out in front of both theatre audience and onstage audience, is highly significant, coming as it does after Prospero's solemn and impressive speech renouncing his magic; he stands before us in finery which intimidates Caliban as 'the wronged Duke of Milan ... a living Prince' who ensures even before the business of reunion gets under way that the courtiers recognize his claim. In the light of this, the forthcoming marriage of Ferdinand and Miranda, to which Prospero and the rest look forward at the play's ending, has extra importance, as a dynastic union between two states. 'Was Milan thrust from Milan that his issue/Should become Kings of Naples?' (V.1.205–6), asks Gonzalo rhetorically.

Ferdinand is crown prince of Naples, and takes this inheritance seriously; believing his father drowned he is at once aware of his own new position – 'myself am Naples' – and he has it at the forefront of his mind when proposing to Miranda:

> *O, if a virgin,*
> *And your affection not gone forth, I'll make you*
> *The Queen of Naples.*

> (I.2.448–50)

He tells her later, in plainer terms, what he is:

> *I am, in my condition,*
> *A prince, Miranda; I do think, a King –*
> *I would not so –*

> (III.1.59–61)

This evident consciousness by Ferdinand of his royal identity is Shake-speare's way of showing the true prince fitted for his role both by birth and by nature; Ferdinand, like Hal in *Henry IV, Part 2*, anticipates his future role, but in each case the eagerness to try out a kingly identity suggests not vaulting ambition but a proper sense of the responsibilities of royal blood and a truly regal vitality. The marriage of Ferdinand and Miranda will unite Milan and Naples, and provide a securer basis for the power which Prospero has striven to regain.

Even on his desert island, Prospero is still a prince, although Caliban mocks his decline in power:

> *I am all the subjects that you have,*
> *Which first was mine own king ...*

> (I.2.341–3)

Though some colonialist interpreters of *The Tempest* have chosen to see in this and some other references evidence for the idea of Prospero as a usurping colonizer who lands on the island from a distant country and by force deprives the native inhabitant, Caliban, of what is rightfully his, this is very much Caliban's viewpoint and not one which the play as a whole will support. For one thing, Caliban is no more a true native than is Miranda, and his claim that 'this island's mine, by Sycorax my mother' does not support his right to rule it. Sycorax, as Prospero has recounted to Ariel a few lines earlier, has been banished from Algiers for sorcery and abandoned, pregnant, on the island by sailors; she asserts her power over Ariel, imprisoning him in a cloven pine when he refuses to obey her 'earthy and abhorr'd commands', but this is limited power, only for evil. And when Caliban is left alone after his mother's death, he is even less fitted to rule than she, lacking her supernatural powers and at the same time being servile by nature. This innate servility is demonstrated clearly in Caliban's reaction to the second group of human beings he encounters on the island, Stephano and Trinculo. His first feeling towards them is fear, when he believes them to be spirits sent from Prospero to punish him, and his second one is instinctive self-abasement:

> *These be fine things, an if they be not sprites.*
> *That's a brave god, and bears celestial liquor.*
> *I will kneel to him.*

(II.2.114–16)

He unquestioningly believes the unscrupulous Stephano's cynical claim to have come from the moon, and only too readily offers himself as slave: 'I'll kiss thy foot; I'll swear myself thy subject'. When the project to kill Prospero and take over the island is hatched at Caliban's instigation, he plans all along for Stephano to be king; his own role is to be 'for aye thy foot-licker' (IV.1.219). Here, if anywhere in this play, is Shakespeare's vision of the colonialist situation, with Stephano and Trinculo as the exploitative travellers from the old world eager for power and self-aggrandisement, completely unconcerned with matters of natural rights, and quick to use the naivety of the native inhabitants for their own ends, while Caliban is one version of the European conception of the Indian, semi-bestial, full of animal cunning, and all too ready a victim of the Europeans' gift of alcohol.

Prospero behaves on the island like a prince because he is a natural ruler. His assumption of authority when he lands is presented to us in such a way that it does not invite critical judgement. When he identifies himself to the still incredulous courtiers in Act V, Scene 1, he asserts what must be taken as truth:

> *... Howsoe'er you have*
> *Been justled from your senses, know for certain*
> *That I am Prospero, and that very Duke*
> *Which was thrust forth of Milan, who most strangely*
> *Upon this shore, where you were wracked, was landed*
> *To be the lord on't ...*

(V.1.157–62)

As lord of this poor kingdom he learns anew the arts of power which he did not sufficiently command as Duke of Milan; the temptation to set aside the sometimes unpleasant demands of government in favour of a retreat into the world of the mind is with him almost to the last, as is evident in Act IV, Scene 1, when he temporarily ignores Caliban's conspiracy in order to concentrate his efforts on the betrothal masque of spirits for Ferdinand and Miranda. He remembers this hateful plot only at the last moment and his composure is totally disrupted. Miranda remarks on her father's extraordinary perturbation: 'Never till this day/ Saw I him touch'd with anger, so distemper'd.'

The recollection of Caliban's ingratitude seems to be one of the things that so disturbs Prospero; it is a failure he cannot reconcile himself to or forget, that despite all his care and tuition Caliban's natural viciousness cannot be overcome. He regains his equanimity, however, when he has the situation under control, and has overcome his own passions to the point where he can even accept the advice of Ariel in treating his enemies with mercy rather than justice. This shows the development of another kind of power in Prospero – power over the self.

> *Though with their high wrongs I am struck to th' quick,*
> *Yet with my nobler reason 'gainst my fury*
> *Do I take part. The rarer action is*
> *In virtue than in vengeance.*

(V.1.25–8)

His learning has educated not only his mind but also his heart; 'fury' and 'vengeance' would be natural reactions for a man who has been treated by his brother as Prospero has, but Prospero is able to subdue these instincts and exercise a higher and rarer quality, forbearance. It was a common view in this period that the prince, to be master of other men, must first be master of himself; to regulate their passions and appetites, he must be able to regulate his own. This moment in the play is the final demonstration of Prospero's achievement of true princely power and full humanity.

The nature of power as a theme in the play is further developed through the contrasting presentation of Prospero's two servants, Ariel and Caliban, and Prospero's relations with them. Ariel, one of Shakespeare's most original and fascinating creations, has many facets. His name was fairly common for a spirit in magical and occult works, and the sound of it does of course suggest that he is 'an ayrie spirit', as he is called in the 'Names of the Actors', though Cornelius Agrippa (*De Occulta Philosophia* II, i; III, xxiv, cited in the Arden edition of *The Tempest* p. 142) uses the name for the chief spirit of the element of earth. Ariel is a servant of the mind rather than the body, and acts as the medium for the exercise of Prospero's magical powers. This both prevents Prospero from the indignity of ever actually conjuring, as other stage-magicians (for example Greene's Friar Bacon in *Friar Bacon and Friar Bungay* and Marlowe's Dr Faustus) do, and also endows Ariel with very great power and responsibility. Ariel is a trusted spirit, and greatly loved by his master whose epithets for him imply a delighted recognition of this servant's peculiar qualities: 'my bird', 'my chick', 'my delicate Ariel', 'my industrious servant', 'my brave spirit', 'my dainty Ariel', 'my tricksy spirit', 'my diligence'. Though for the purposes of the play he must be physically embodied, Ariel is obviously to be regarded as immaterial. His first speeches, where he describes how he has enacted the storm Prospero commanded – 'performed' is in fact Prospero's word for it – emphasize his qualities as a shape-changer:

> *I boarded the King's ship. Now on the beak,*
> *Now in the waist, the deck, in every cabin*
> *I flamed amazement. Sometime I'd divide,*
> *And burn in many places. On the topmast,*
> *The yards, and boresprit would I flame distinctly,*
> *Then meet and join.*

(I.2.196–201)

He can move so fast that he makes Puck's promise to Oberon to 'put a girdle round about the earth in forty minutes' sound almost leaden: 'I drink the air before me, and return/Or ere your pulse twice beat.'

At times it is as if Prospero can think Ariel into being and the master's will is perfected in the servant's action. Unlike Puck, Ariel makes no mistakes, and nothing he is commanded to do causes him any effort. Yet there is another side to this master–servant relationship, which Shakespeare presents to us early in the play. Like more conventional spirit-servants in other plays, Ariel has his moods of bad temper and reluctance when he has to be forced back into line and he is careful to remind Prospero that their relationship is based on a bargain:

> *I prithee,*
> *Remember I have done thee worthy service,*
> *Told thee no lies, made no mistakings, served*
> *Without or grudge or grumblings. Thou did promise*
> *To bate me a full year.*

(I.2.246–50)

Prospero must assert himself here, as master, and remind his servant of the gulf that divides them:

> *If thou more murmur'st, I will rend an oak,*
> *And peg thee in his knotty entrails, till*
> *Thou hast howled away twelve winters.*

(I.2.294–6)

Ariel is duly quelled by this threat and Prospero's confirmation of the promise of imminent freedom brings out in him a childlike eagerness to be as good a servant as possible for the remainder of his time:

> *That's my noble master!*
> *What shall I do? Say what! What shall I do?*

This aspect of the relationship, though drawing upon the convention that a magician has to enforce his power over his spirits by constant vigilance and that they might often show reluctance to obey, serves an important function in humanizing Prospero and in creating a poignancy about their impending separation. For Prospero not only appreciates Ariel as a servant, but he loves him too, and the bond between them is stronger than any feeling Prospero has for another human being. Naturally Prospero cherishes Miranda, and she returns his love, mingled with an awe towards her powerful and mysterious parent, but Shakespeare does not show any affinity of nature between them, and in comparison with other daughter-figures like Imogen or Marina, Miranda's barely sketched character is little more than that of a very young and inexperienced girl. Between Prospero and Ariel, however, there is an affinity so close that it is sometimes as if Ariel exists as a faculty of Prospero's mind, his imagination personified. 'Come with a thought' is Prospero's invocation (IV.1.164) and Ariel answers, 'Thy thoughts I cleave to'. Prospero frequently praises Ariel for carrying out his tasks so well, and delights in the supreme skills of the spirit, on which he relies to fulfil his plan. He loves Ariel; and the pain of his knowledge that the spirit cannot return his feeling (for Ariel has only intellectual comprehension of human affections) is delicately implicit in the scene in Act V where after Ariel has sung his song of freedom, 'Where the bee sucks, there suck I', Prospero comments sadly, 'Why, that's my dainty Ariel! I shall miss thee,/But yet thou shalt have freedom'.

The relationship between Prospero and Caliban seems on the surface quite antithetical to this, and yet it might again be called a master–servant relationship strengthened by a deeper bond. Where Prospero depends on Ariel's spirit-powers to carry out his magic, he depends on Caliban to supply humble physical needs; the hated slave, feared by Miranda whom he has tried to rape, is essential to the household.

> *... As 'tis,*
> *We cannot miss him. He does make our fire,*
> *Fetch in our wood, and serves in offices*
> *That profit us.*

(I.2.310–13)

55

Caliban has acquired survival skills and certain refinements beyond this; he takes a considerable pleasure in them when he offers to demonstrate his special services to Stephano:

> *I prithee, let me bring thee where crabs grow;*
> *And I with my long nails will dig thee pignuts,*
> *Show thee a jay's nest, and instruct thee how*
> *To snare the nimble marmoset. I'll bring thee*
> *To clust'ring filberts, and sometimes I'll get thee*
> *Young scamels from the rock.*

(II.2.164–9)

Prospero shows no recognition that Caliban has any talents at all; in fact, he is bitter towards the monster because Caliban has rejected or perverted all the gifts his master has tried to offer him. Prospero and Miranda extend to Caliban the benefits of civilization, in particular, shelter in their cell, human society, and the gift of language. But his inherently bestial nature prevents Caliban from taking advantage of these benefits; he is so incurably vile in his behaviour that Prospero and Miranda cannot endure to be with him, and his only profit, so he says, from learning to speak is the ability to curse. He hates Prospero, and resents having to serve him, but has to do so out of fear; Prospero controls Caliban by threats of physical torment. Exchanges between them commonly take the form of cursing and insults. Prospero calls Caliban by such terms as 'thou prisoner slave', 'lying slave', 'abhorred slave', 'brutish', 'villain', 'filth', 'hag-seed' and 'thing of darkness', while Caliban invokes on his master 'All the charms of Sycorax, toads, beetles, bats', 'all the infections that the sun sucks up' as well as plagues and sickness. Caliban's abusive language is to be expected in a sub-human being but the sustained virulence of Prospero's speech is surprising. It is not uncommon for magicians in plays to curse their enemies, but for Prospero to do it so much and in such terms seems to suggest an earthbound side to his nature. His language of malevolence sometimes recalls fairy magic and the spells of witches rather than the scholarly terminology of a spiritually refined magus, but perhaps we are to see the low curses as appropriate to the low nature of the cursed. Caliban's animal being cannot be radically changed; he is 'a savage and deformed slave' and neither Prospero's magic arts nor his human efforts can alter this condition, a lesson which it hurts him to learn. The surface meaning of Prospero's words to the courtiers in Act V when Caliban, Stephano and Trinculo are driven in wearing their stolen finery is that Caliban is not of the court party:

> Two of these fellows you
> Must know and own. This thing of darkness I
> Acknowledge mine.
>
> (V.1.274–6)

But we see a bitter acceptance here of Prospero's responsibility for this creature; it is worth contrasting the cool tone of these words with the anguished bitterness of Prospero's outbreak against Caliban in Act IV:

> A devil, a born devil, on whose nature
> Nurture can never stick; on whom my pains,
> Humanely taken, all, all lost, quite lost.
>
> (IV.1.188–90)

Prospero has privately conquered his own passions, and with the ability to pardon his enemies he finds also that resignation of spirit to accept what must be.

The Tempest shows us that there are some natures which cannot be improved by nurture. Nature, the natural state, is polarized against nurture, that state of being without civility, art or grace. In Caliban it is not a condition of blessed innocence, uncorrupted by society, nor a state of moral neutrality. Caliban's inherent propensity is for evil. His instincts are to satisfy appetite and to avoid discomfort, and to do these things he will lie, betray kindness, and cheat and abase himself to any extent, as is demonstrated in the situations which arise when he encounters Stephano and Trinculo. First of all he succumbs to the 'celestial liquor' which Stephano has managed to preserve, and is ready to become Stephano's slave to ensure a continued supply. He thinks that escaping from Prospero will give him freedom, and cannot understand that he is merely transferring himself from one kind of servitude to another. He is cunning enough to tell lies and flatter Stephano into the project of murdering Prospero and taking over the isle, but too cowardly to confront his master face to face or do the deed himself; his brutishness delights in the contemplating of the killing:

> ... As I told thee, 'tis a custom with him
> I'th' afternoon to sleep. There thou mayst brain him,
> Having first seized his books; or with a log
> Batter his skull, or paunch him with a stake,
> Or cut his weasand with a knife.
>
> (III.2.88–92)

When, on the way to Prospero's cell to commit the murder, the three of them are confronted by the 'glistering apparel' Ariel has produced to distract them, only Caliban is not taken in. So intent is he on doing away with his master and freeing himself forever from Prospero's punishments that he can despise the clothing as 'trash' and 'luggage'. This shows the single-minded intensity of his hatred for Prospero rather than superior powers of discrimination. Stephano and Trinculo, easily sidetracked into squabbling and pilfering, take the projected murder much less seriously than Caliban; they have not his desire for revenge to spur them on. Thus Prospero's attempt to 'nurture' Caliban is ill-rewarded, and the instinct of the monster for all that is dark and violent thwarted only by the exercise of intellect and magic art. It may be objected that Caliban's ability to respond to the 'sounds and sweet airs' of the isle implies a spiritual potentiality and sensitivity. Certainly, he is for a moment elevated above the dully materialist Stephano who comments crudely on Caliban's description of the mysterious harmonies, 'This will prove a brave kingdom to me, where I shall have my music for nothing', but the ability to respond to music was then thought to be an attribute of beasts which lacked reason, and need not indicate the presence of a higher nature in Caliban.

Nature in Miranda is capable of improvement; because she is of noble blood she can learn from Prospero's tuition, and the combination of her own inherent qualities with the education she is given by her scholar-father make her a fit wife for a future king although she has no experience of civilized society. Prospero's praise of her to Ferdinand should not be interpreted either as conventional hyperbole or fond paternal pride:

> *O Ferdinand,*
> *Do not smile at me that I boast her off,*
> *For thou shalt find she will outstrip all praise,*
> *And make it halt behind her.*

(IV.1.8–11)

She is both innocent and refined, and despite her ignorance of the world capable of discriminating judgement. The couple are hardly drawn at all as 'characters', but clearly they are meant to complement one another as versions of innocence and experience, nature and civilization; Ferdinand as a young prince has seen and known all sorts of women, while Miranda has never met a man other than her father, yet the two are aware of an instant affinity. He is society perfected and not corrupted, as she is nature refined and not bestial. That society is capable of corruption as much as nature is evident in the court party and their retainers. Stephano and

Trinculo, Antonio and Sebastian are of the noblest blood yet inexplicably wicked, and it is not clear if they are penitent at the end. Antonio is another of Shakespeare's mismatched siblings, like Don Pedro's villainous brother Don John in *Much Ado*, or Edmund in *King Lear*, who confronts the world with an hereditary enigma; 'Good wombs have borne bad sons', says Miranda helplessly when Prospero tells her the story of Antonio's treachery and asks, rhetorically, for some explanation of it:

> *Mark his condition and th' event; then tell me*
> *If this might be a brother.*

(I.2.117–18)

Antonio shares Prospero's blood, and, presumably, his upbringing and circumstances, but these things cannot save him from the corruption of ambition. Ultimate evil is always represented in Shakespeare as the betrayal of the bonds of nature, usually in the form of kinship. Not only does Antonio never express any remorse for his behaviour towards Prospero, he actually encourages Sebastian to imitate it in disposing of his brother, Alonso. Sebastian is almost equally lacking in scruples. It does occur to him to wonder whether Antonio's conscience might trouble him, but he is completely overruled by Antonio's vigorous and cynical reply:

SEBASTIAN: *But, for your conscience?*
ANTONIO: *Ay, sir, where lies that? If 'twere a kibe,*
> *'Twould put me to my slipper; but I feel not*
> *This deity in my bosom. Twenty consciences*
> *That stand 'twixt me and Milan, candied be they,*
> *And melt ere they molest.*

(II.1.280–85)

Antonio's mocking term for conscience, 'this deity', at once recognizes and rejects the traditional idea of the guardian spirit, the Faustian Good Angel, the divinely instituted mentor and guide, and Sebastian is convinced by Antonio's forceful speech. Sebastian's brother, Alonso, who has been equally guilty of unscrupulous machinations to wrest power away from Prospero, is so overcome with remorse when Ariel confronts 'three men of sin' with their crimes that he feels himself accused by the whole natural world:

> *O, it is monstrous, monstrous!*
> *Methought the billows spoke, and told me of it;*

> *The winds did sing it to me; and the thunder,*
> *That deep and dreadful organ-pipe, pronounced*
> *The name of Prosper: it did bass my trespass.*

> (III.3.97–101)

Truly penitent, Alonso is at the end of the play truly forgiven, but there is no obvious mark of these things in Antonio and Sebastian, who are perhaps like Caliban, irreclaimably corrupt.

Stephano and Trinculo occupy an intermediate position between Caliban and the courtiers. As a butler and a jester they are court servants, but they are low, unrefined figures, untouched by the better aspects of civilized life, and susceptible to the temptations that the island has to offer. Drunken bombastic Stephano is the more fully realized, in his readiness to exploit Caliban's simplicity, and his unthinking acceptance of brutality. He is bawdy and intemperate, a would-be king who cannot control his own appetites, let alone those of any subjects. The animal side of his nature is in no way tamed or modified by society, but he has none of the high spirits and good humour of Shakespeare's other lovers of belly-cheer, like Falstaff and Sir Toby Belch. He is gross and charmless, without the gifts of either nature or nurture. His half-baked plot to kill Prospero and take over the island parodies the more calculating murderousness of Antonio and Sebastian; it has the function of a comic subplot, but the behaviour of Stephano and Trinculo is too spiritless and sordid ever to be funny. Trinculo, the court jester, is as out of place on the island as Lear's fool on the heath, but he has none of the other's intuitive wit. The demise of the plot when the conspirators are first of all tricked by Ariel into a filthy pond, and finally hunted down and physically tormented by spirits in the shape of dogs, is appropriately designed for the humiliation of such low beings. There is something perfunctory in Shakespeare's handling of these figures and the comic subplot of the play; they fulfil their part in the total scheme but they do no more than that. They have no independent life, and they shrink away, shamefaced, when confronted at the end by their master.

In some ways the view of life in the play may appear a rather desolate one, yet in treating themes of forgiveness and redemption Shakespeare also offers a positive vision. Instead of depicting long years of the separation of kinsfolk, as in *Pericles* or *The Winter's Tale*, Shakespeare shows the culmination of the events of twelve years in a few hours of compressed action, in which enemies are reconciled and crimes pardoned. The period of time that has elapsed between the initial event that set the sequence of events in motion, that is Antonio's and Alonso's usurption of Prospero, and the present is not an arbitrary space but a length sufficient for a new generation to reach adulthood. The fact that Prospero and Alonso both have children now of marriageable age alters the situation in two ways: a whole cycle in the process of human life has come round and the question of who rules Milan and Naples now has a future perspective. Time is therefore ripe for the matter to be reopened. Fortune collaborates with Prospero in helping deliver his enemies into his hands, by sending them off-course on their return journey from Tunis to Italy, after the celebration of Claribel's wedding; Prospero by his art completes the process in raising the storm that shipwrecks them onto his island. Once there, he subjects them to a series of trials and torments which confuse their perceptions and baffle them before he confronts them in person.

The culmination of this process is in Act III, Scene 3, where Prospero conjures up a magical banquet to tempt the court party. This symbol of hospitality so welcome and delicious to the weary travellers, and so mysteriously produced by 'strange shapes' speechlessly inviting them to taste, is amazing to all of the party; even Antonio sees this vision as a proof that the fabulous can also be true. The spirit-shapes silently vanish and the travellers pause uneasily; then Alonso, the most heart-sick and despairing of them, feeling there is nothing to lose, prepares to eat: 'I will stand to and feed,/Although my last – no matter, since I feel/The best is past', he says, perhaps with the underlying implication that this may be a diabolic banquet which will condemn his soul to the underworld if he tastes it. Immediately there is thunder and lightning, Ariel appears like a harpy, and the banquet is gone. Ariel's disguise here has classical origins; in Homer and Virgil harpies were monstrous creatures with the faces of beautiful women but the bodies of birds, who are represented as rapaciously devouring. His words, however, express Christian ideas about sin, guilt and punishment; the connection between the crimes of these 'three men of sin' and their present situation is a direct one:

> *... Remember –*
> *For that's my business to you – that you three*
> *From Milan did supplant good Prospero,*
> *Exposed unto the sea, which hath requit it,*
> *Him and his innocent child; for which foul deed*
> *The powers, delaying, not forgetting, have*
> *Incensed the seas and shores, yea, all the creatures*
> *Against your peace.*

(III.3.69–76)

Ariel points out not only the nature of the punishment but also the way to atonement; he is the mouthpiece of retribution but has words also to offer hope. Continuing in their present course of life will result in 'lingering perdition – worse than any death/Can be at once', but the angry powers are not implacable, and 'heart's sorrow and a clear life ensuing' can save them from this fate. The men of sin react in different ways to Ariel's impressive speech, Sebastian and Antonio dashing off to fight fiends with the bravado of desperation, and Alonso so overcome by consciousness of guilt that he wants only to die. Gonzalo, who is able to speak objectively, comments that this behaviour is only the beginning of a process:

> All three of them are desperate. Their great guilt,
> Like poison given to work a great time after,
> Now 'gins to bite their spirits.

(III.3.106–8)

The image he uses, of the delayed action of poison, could imply the spiritual fatality of guilt; but Ariel has hinted strongly at a favourable outcome of events, and since we know already that Alonso has not been punished so finally as he thinks by the death of Ferdinand, we are prepared for a conclusion in which things will work out well.

The final scene follows a pattern set by the other romances, though *The Tempest* has significant variations. All the participants in the action find themselves unexpectedly thrown together after adventures and a long journey, with the exception of course of Prospero who is the agent and contriver of this reunion. Those thought dead are discovered to be alive; a lost child is restored to a joyous parent; those who have committed offences repent and are pardoned. The stress of the final scene falls on these positive elements; of the court party, Alonso and Gonzalo are the most vocal, and each responds affirmatively when Prospero steps forward in his ducal robes. Alonso is the first, ready, even glad, to beg Prospero's pardon and give up his claim to tribute from the dukedom of Milan even before he is quite certain of Prospero's identity. Already he begins to feel an abatement of his guilt and spiritual torment: '... since I saw thee,/Th'affliction of my mind amends, with which/I fear a madness held me' (V.1.114–16). The spotlight remains on Alonso when Prospero makes his next move, revealing Ferdinand and Miranda at chess within his cell. The genuineness of Alonso's spiritual renewal is testified to in the way he reacts to the recovery of Ferdinand, whom he had believed dead, asking his forgiveness. The language in this part of the play brings a religious quality to the action:

SEBASTIAN:	*A most high miracle.*
FERDINAND:	*Though the seas threaten, they are merciful.*
	I have cursed them without cause.
ALONSO:	*Now all the blessings*
	Of a glad father compass thee about!

(V.1.177–80)

Once Alonso has realized the need for Ferdinand's forgiveness as well as Prospero's, Prospero puts an end to the expression of his guilt, suggesting that his need for self-recrimination and punishment is at an end:

> *There, sir, stop.*
> *Let us not burden our remembrances with*
> *A heaviness that's gone.*

(V.1.198–200)

Now it is Gonzalo's turn; he is an old man, his responses accordingly slower, and he has not Alonso's guilt and pressing need to atone. From the position of a benign observer he draws a joyous meaning from the outcome of events, which Alonso confirms:

GONZALO:	*I have inly wept,*
	Or should have spoke ere this. Look down, you gods,
	And on this couple drop a blessèd crown!
	For it is you that have chalked forth the way
	Which brought us hither.
ALONSO:	*I say, Amen, Gonzalo.*
GONZALO:	*Was Milan thrust from Milan that his issue*
	Should become kings of Naples? O, rejoice
	Beyond a common joy, and set it down
	With gold on lasting pillars. In one voyage
	Did Claribel her husband find at Tunis,
	And Ferdinand her brother found a wife
	Where he himself was lost; Prospero his dukedom
	In a poor isle, and all of us ourselves
	When no man was his own.

(V.1.200–213)

Behind Gonzalo's words seems to lie the Christian idea of the *felix culpa* or Fortunate Fall, the paradox whereby a sinful act may be reversed through the exercise of God's providence, and result in a happy and blessed outcome which demonstrates the power for good of the Creator. It is perhaps the strongest expression of that universal sense of good coming from evil found at the end of each of the romances. But we should be careful to notice how Shakespeare avoids too facile an optimism. The most rapturous expression of delight is Miranda's exclamation at the 'brave new world' she imagines as she first sees the rulers and courtiers of Naples and Milan. It is poignant that we should question such rapture, but it is crucial to Shakespeare's effect that we realize the people Miranda apostrophizes have acted wickedly and that not all of them have fully reformed. None the less, the rejoicing of Alonso and Gonzalo seems to include everyone present, and the mood of amazed delight at good fortune is contained in the next moments, when Ariel brings in the Master and Boatswain from Alonso's vessel, who have not been seen since they seemed about to drown in the play's first scene. They bring yet more good tidings, that the ship

> *Which, but three glasses since, we gave out split –*
> *Is tight and yare and bravely rigged, as when*
> *We first put out to sea.*

(V.1.223–5)

One of the last pieces of the pattern falls into place with the appearance of Caliban, Stephano and Trinculo, drunk and discomfited in their stolen finery. They cannot be expected to participate in the general happiness on a high level, but they respond with proper humility, and Caliban, in a simple way, acknowledges his mistakes:

> *I'll be wise hereafter,*
> *And seek for grace. What a thrice double ass*
> *Was I to take this drunkard for a god,*
> *And worship this dull fool!*

(V.1.295–8)

They too are restored to their appropriate places in the scheme planned and sanctioned by Prospero. The one character who seems not to be fitted in is Antonio. Prospero singles him out for pardon early in the scene, in a speech that has sometimes been thought cold:

> *For you, most wicked sir, whom to call brother*
> *Would even infect my mouth, I do forgive*
> *Thy rankest fault – all of them; and require*
> *My dukedom of thee, which perforce, I know,*
> *Thou must restore.*

(V.1.130–34)

Antonio is given no word of reply, and in fact has only one speech in the rest of the play, a sneering comment on Caliban's freakishness. Since he is the character who has sinned most greatly against Prospero it would be fascinating to know what reaction Shakespeare meant for him here. But whether we take his silence for unrepentance or interpret it as a kind of wordless, perhaps shamed, acceptance of Prospero's forgiveness, it is clear that Shakespeare does not dwell on the reconciliation of the brothers or the penitence of Antonio as he does on, say, the penitence of Iachimo in *Cymbeline* or Leontes in *The Winter's Tale*. The play ends with Prospero's promise of good weather for the return voyage to Milan and his farewell to Ariel, who will be the only one not to go. The court party then retire into Prospero's cell for the night to hear the rest of his story. This, of course, is the story that we already know, which gives a satisfyingly conclusive feel to the play's ending. A cycle is complete. This is where we came in.

It would be wrong, however, to summarize *The Tempest*'s overall impression as one of conclusiveness or finality, for one of the play's most characteristic qualities is its celebration of transience and impermanence. 'Celebration' may seem an unexpected term when the play's most significant expression of the scheme of transience is Prospero's speech of regret for the passing of beautiful appearances in the wedding-masque scene, but there are several ways in which kinds of changeability and illusion are specifically exploited for their own virtues. Ariel, for instance, who constantly reappears in different guises, is a spirit without bodily substance whose nature is one of fleeting appearances and changing forms. He takes whatever shape is required by his mission of the moment; he is totally adaptable to circumstance. Most often he appears with music, singing to enchant Ferdinand or evoke the delightful prospect of freedom, lulling the courtiers to sleep with solemn harmonies, bewildering Stephano and Trinculo with eerie piping. Though Ariel is a spirit of the intellect, over whom Prospero has control because of his own scholarship and spiritual attainment, the music which is the medium of his influence on human behaviour acts on the feelings, not the conscious mind. It may represent the mysterious workings of the imagination, or what the Elizabethans would call the 'fantasy'. Although music in a play may be used to symbolize harmony and order, as in *The Merchant of Venice* (Act V, Scene 1) for instance, it can also be an agent of alluring illusion; the magical songs Ariel sings to Ferdinand tell misleadingly of death and transformation, for Ferdinand's father is by no means buried 'full fathom five'. Music has the power to change atmosphere and mood; Ferdinand finds himself caught in its spell:

> *... Sitting on a bank,*
> *Weeping again the King my father's wrack,*
> *This music crept by me upon the waters,*
> *Allaying both their fury and my passion*
> *With its sweet air ...*

(I.2.390–94)

Stephano and Trinculo – who have their own low-life drinking songs which parody it – are terrified by Ariel's music, but Caliban is reassured by it. Indeed, his response to the 'sweet airs' suggests how Shakespeare makes Caliban, for all his greater evil, evoke poetic responses in us in a way that the villains to whom he allies himself do not. Music is a part of all the play's spectacular set-pieces too, and the use of stage-spectacle is another means of embodying the idea of transience.

The Tempest is one of the most reliant of Shakespeare's plays on visual spectacle and the unusually full stage-directions, which some scholars consider may be a later addition to Shakespeare's original, suggest a masque-like elaboration in the use of costume, music and scenic devices. Some of the spectacles are short-lived, and there is a kind of prodigality about their staging. The banquet in Act III, Scene 3, which has been called 'Shakespeare's most elaborate experiment in stage-spectacle', requires music, a number of 'strange shapes', and a 'quaint device' or ingenious mechanism by means of which Ariel with his harpy's wings can cause the spread to disappear; the masque in Act IV, Scene 1 needs quite a large, richly costumed cast of nymphs and reapers to dance, as well as three goddesses of which at least one sings and descends to the stage from above. On both occasions the spectacle must disappear very suddenly. There may well have been some visual effects to suggest the storm at sea in the opening scene of the play, and perhaps also the labouring ship. Thunderstorm effects are several times called for in the course of the action. Prospero's cave or cell could, of course, have been very simply represented, but it is also possible that for the production at court in 1611 he might have had some Renaissance-style grotto as envisaged by the French scholar and garden designer Salomon De Caus who planned gardens with fantastic caves and grottoes at Somerset House in Greenwich and at Richmond Palace in this period for Anne of Denmark.

The degree of simplicity or sophistication of stage design in *The Tempest* must, of course, depend on the place and conditions in which the play was put on, and since it was probably performed in three theatres, the Blackfriars, the Globe, and the Cockpit, as well as at court between 1611 and 1613 (when the Globe was destroyed by fire) it had to be adaptable.

None the less, it is not far-fetched to see how the poignant expression of transience in Prospero's 'our revels now are ended' speech, with its use of theatrical terminology and its impressionistic vision of 'the cloud-capped towers, the gorgeous palaces, the solemn temples' of worldly magnificence might be emphasized and given an extra significance by the visual spectacle of theatrical illusion. Our delight in the beauty of stage contrivances is enhanced by the miraculous power by which they may be instantly transformed as well as by our awareness of their insubstantiality. In his multi-layered presentation of theatrical art Shakespeare shows Prospero both as a kind of creator, an author-surrogate, contriving and organizing the whole of the action, the total extent and meaning of his control only gradually emerging in the course of the play, and finally also as an actor, a puppet manipulated in his turn by the playwright and dependent upon the audience's response for the success of the fiction. In the epilogue Shakespeare returns to the imagery of magic, but here Prospero, making the transition between his role in the play and his function as an actor, represents himself as a being without power. Magic is metaphorically used of the actor's art, which he is in the process of abandoning, his part in the play having come to an end:

> *Now my charms are all o'erthrown,*
> *And what strength I have's mine own,*
> *Which is most faint.*

Now it is the audience which takes on the role of conjurer or magician with power to transform the situation:

> *Let me not,*
> *Since I have my dukedom got*
> *And pardoned the deceiver, dwell*
> *In this bare island by your spell;*
> *But release me from my bands*
> *With the help of your good hands.*
> *Gentle breath of yours my sails*
> *Must fill, or else my project fails,*
> *Which was to please. Now I want*
> *Spirits to enforce, art to enchant.*

The audience's willingness to applaud the spectacle, and thus confirm the actor's success, will be equivalent to the gesture Prospero made at the ending of the play, rounding off his project by providing a good wind for the voyage home. The actor's project is correspondingly humbler than Prospero's – he wants only to please, and he has now no 'spirits' or 'art' to achieve this. The last lines revert to the Christian ideas that have underlain Prospero's decision to pardon rather than punish his enemies; the actor prays for the audience's forbearance and mercy towards his failings, reminding them that we should forgive others as we wish to be forgiven ourselves.

Criticism of *The Tempest*

The earliest piece of criticism of *The Tempest* is probably to be found in Ben Jonson's comic induction to his play *Bartholomew Fair* (1614) in which the Scrivener, or professional copyist for the company, supposedly warning the audience of what to expect and what not to expect in the play, is made to defend it and its author against those who would compare it with Shakespeare's romances:

> *If there be never a servant-monster i' the Fair, who can help it? He* [i.e. Jonson, the playwright] *says; or a nest of antics? He is loth to make nature afraid in his plays, like those that beget* Tales, Tempests, *and such like drolleries.*

> (*Works*, ed. Herford and Simpson, VI, 16)

Jonson, through the mouthpiece of his character, scorns Shakespeare's late plays for their basis in fantasy and romance, and their lack of realistic and satiric elements fundamental to his own comedy, implying a vulgar appeal to unrefined popular taste. There is, certainly, evidence to suggest that Shakespeare's romances, particularly *Pericles*, were successful at the box-office, but their performances at court imply an appeal of another sort. Jonson's criticism does, however, anticipate objections to the romances from neo-classical critics of the later seventeenth and eighteenth centuries, although *The Tempest* consistently finds more favour than the others. Dryden mentions the lame plots and 'ridiculous, incoherent story' of *Pericles* and *The Winter's Tale* (*Essays*, ed. W. Ker, 1, 165) but admires *The Tempest*, and singles out the characterization of the 'servant-monster' Caliban for special praise, as a triumph of poetic invention. He was echoed in this by Addison, in the *Spectator* of 19 January 1712:

> *It shows a greater Genius in* Shakespeare *to have drawn his* Calyban, *than his* Hotspur *or* Julius Caesar. *The one was to be supplied out of his own imagination, whereas the other might have been formed upon Tradition, History and Observation.*

Critics and editors of Shakespeare in the eighteenth century consistently admired the poetic fancy of *The Tempest*, especially since it existed in combination with an attention unusual for Shakespeare to the unities of time, place and plot. Dr Johnson remarked with approval that 'its plan is regular', and also praised the 'boundless invention' of character and action, but he found less to admire in the other romances, and excluded *Pericles* completely from his edition of Shakespeare. This was the general practice of eighteenth-century editors, and it should also be remembered that when the plays were staged during this time it was almost always in a regularized and 'improved' version which omitted features like the masque of Jupiter in *Cymbeline* or the betrothal masque of spirits in *The Tempest.* Dryden and Davenant's version was generally preferred to Shakespeare's until Macready reintroduced the original play in 1838.

As neo-classical tastes in drama began to be superseded in the later eighteenth century with the rise of the Romantic movement, so *The Tempest* began to be valued for other qualities; less importance was attached to its observation of the unities and correspondingly more to its imaginative inventiveness. Joseph Warton, writing in *The Adventurer*, 93 (1753), praises its amazing wildness of fancy:

Of all the plays of Shakespeare, The Tempest *is the most striking instance of his creative power. He has there given the reins to his boundless imagination, and has carried the romantic, the wonderful, and the wild, to the most pleasing extravagance.*

In the nineteenth century the play continued to find favour, although Lamb felt that, like *King Lear*, it was a piece for the imagination rather than the stage, which could not do it justice. Coleridge, one of the play's best critics, seems to have shared this view, because in his praise for the play's special appeal to the imagination he derides the claims of 'mere scenery' for attention, as distracting from the 'spiritual vision' at the heart of the play. According to his theory of poetic literature, what matters is not adherence to neo-classical rules for the sustaining of an illusion of realism but rather the creation of a consistent and autonomous imaginative world; he sees *The Tempest* as a perfect example of the imaginative reality of poetry:

The Tempest ... *has been selected as a specimen of the romantic drama; i.e. of a drama the interests of which are independent of all historical facts and associations, and arise from their fitness to that faculty of our nature, the imagination I mean, which gives no allegiance to time and place.*

Coleridge was one of the first to interpret the play rather than simply admire it, seeing in it an exploration of ideas about the moral being and the conditioning effects of civilization. For him it exemplified Shakespeare's stance as a 'philosophical aristocrat' who delights in hereditary institutions and distinctions of rank as advantages to society as a whole, but never propagandizes for any particular political viewpoint. Coleridge's approach anticipated the twentieth-century concern with concepts of nature and nurture in the play, and its polarizing of nature and society.

The shift from regarding poetry in general and Shakespeare's plays in particular as representations of nature and the external world to seeing them as expressions of the poet's state of mind prepared the way for the allegorizing of Shakespeare's work which is so prominent in the criticism of the later nineteenth century, and subsequently. Ernest Dowden, in *Shakespeare: A Critical Study of his Mind and Art* (1875), put forward a view of the romances as the product of the 'large, serene wisdom' of Shakespeare's own nature as it is revealed in the writing of the last plays, for instance his 'self-mastery, his calm vitality of will ... and ... a certain abandonment, a remoteness from the common joys and sorrows of the world'. This identification leads to an allegorical reading of the play, which Dowden puts forward tentatively, with Prospero as Shakespeare the Artist, Miranda as his Art, Ariel as the genius of Poetry only newly liberated in the Elizabethan age, and Ferdinand as Fletcher, Shakespeare's follower. The editor of the first Arden *Tempest*, Morton Luce, while not endorsing Dowden's allegory in detail, did help to give currency to the autobiographical reading of the play which shows in Prospero an ageing Shakespeare who, 'calm of mind, all passion spent' after the great tragedies, looks beyond the rough magic of his art to a greater fulfilment in the life hereafter. Lytton Strachey in his famous essay 'Shakespeare's Final Period' (1906) reacted strongly against such idealizing of the late plays by debunking them both as works of art and as products of mature contentment, insisting that Shakespeare at the end of his career was 'bored with people, bored with real life, bored with drama, bored, in fact, with everything except poetry and poetical dreams'. Much subsequent criticism has been concerned to find ways of answering Strachey: by treating the romances as a group which deals creatively with post-tragic themes; by considering them in relation to the contemporary context and seventeenth-century theatrical conditions, especially as a response to the rise of the new dramatists Beaumont and Fletcher; by subjecting them to various kinds of mythological and allegorical interpretations and thereby discovering hidden profundities; by relating them to the mode of Romance and its long tradition, from the third-century Greek prose narrative *Daphnis and Chloe* up to Sidney's *Arcadia*.

In the twentieth century the work of Tillyard and of Wilson Knight on the last plays (*Shakespeare's Last Plays* (1938) by Tillyard; *Myth and Miracle* (1929) by Wilson Knight) did much to establish a view of the plays which has become accepted as standard. For those critics they represent 'the final, regenerative phase of the tragic pattern' (Tillyard), 'the culmination of a series' (Wilson Knight), in which the characters, having undergone profoundly tragic experiences of suffering and loss, survive to enjoy a new vision of hope and transcendence. This interpretation is at its most convincing if the plays are treated as a group, and *The Tempest* recapitulates romance-themes found throughout Shakespeare's career; we can note especially the way in which certain favourite symbols, such as storms, voyages, feasts, especially disrupted ones, and music, are used with particular significance in *The Tempest*. This interpretation leads naturally on to an allegorical reading of the play whereby Prospero represents Shakespeare's super-hero, sometimes speaking in Shakespeare's own voice, Ariel his spiritual and imaginative side, and Caliban his animal nature. With variations, this basic scheme (which did not in fact originate with Wilson Knight) has been accepted by many readers, including W. H. Auden in *The Sea and the Mirror*, which he has subtitled 'A Commentary on *The Tempest*'. In a slightly earlier allegorical interpretation, also influential, by Churton Collins in 'Poetry and Symbolism: A Study of *The Tempest*', in the *Contemporary Review* (January 1908), Prospero's island is seen as the world, with Prospero as its ruling divinity: the courtiers who have sinned against him repent and are forgiven, and they represent mankind. Thus the play is taken to demonstrate an optimistic and Christian view of life.

There are many more specific and detailed interpretations, perhaps the most notorious of which is by Colin Still in *Shakespeare's Mystery Play* (1921) and *The Timeless Theme* (1936). Still finds close parallels between the events of the play and the initiation ceremonies of the Eleusinian mysteries, where, for instance, the courtiers follow the pattern of the Lesser Initiation through Purgatory, to which the Ceremony of Water, that is, the shipwreck, is a preliminary. Their revitalized clothing represents their ultimate spiritual redemption. Of all Shakespeare's plays *The Tempest* has lent itself to the widest variety of allegorical readings. Dowden mentions interpretations of Caliban as the People, the understanding without imagination, the missing link between man and apes, the colony of Virginia, and the early drama of Marlowe. A recent view which treats the play as a symbolic rendering of occult and political ideas is that of Frances Yates in *Shakespeare's Last Plays: A New Approach* (1975) and *The Occult Philosophy in the Elizabethan Age* (1979). Yates calls the play 'a Rosicrucian manifesto' and finds evidence in it of Shakespeare's support for the alchemist John Dee, then out of favour with King James, whose art is represented in Prospero's magic; she also sees in it an endorsement of the political revival of Elizabethan values and the Protestant cause, spearheaded by Prince Henry in the period around 1610.

Other twentieth-century critics of Shakespeare have related *The Tempest* to its times in terms of stagecraft. The precise nature of the relationship between the romances as a group and the plays of Beaumont and Fletcher, first investigated by A. Thorndike in *The Influence of Beaumont and Fletcher on Shakespeare* (1901), is uncertain because of the relative dating of *Cymbeline* and Beaumont and Fletcher's *Philaster*, but it is likely that Fletcher's pastoral tragi-comedy, *The Faithful Shepherdess* (1608), influenced the structure and conception of *The Tempest*. Links between *The Tempest* and another important Jacobean theatrical phenomenon, the court masque, have been well established since they were first studied in detail by Enid Welsford in *The Court Masque* (1927), and must be taken into account in any discussion of the play's staging. Suggestive theories of staging in specific locations are to be found in Sir E. Law's Shakespeare Association Pamphlet, 'Shakespeare's *Tempest* as originally produced at Court' (1920), and J. C. Adams, *The Globe Playhouse* (1943).

Another aspect of the late plays as a group to stimulate recent interpretation has been their mode as Romance. For some critics this has meant relating them to a long tradition of narrative going back to the Greeks, which has for its subject-matter stories of quests, journeys and strange adventures undertaken by a hero in far-away countries and far-off times. The particular forms taken by romance in Elizabethan literature were the long narrative in prose or verse, such as Sidney's *Arcadia* or Spenser's *The Faerie Queene*, or romantic drama like Greene's *Friar Bacon and Friar Bungay*, Peele's *The Old Wives Tale*, and *Mucedorus*. The affinities between Shakespeare's late plays and this tradition have been examined by Howard Felperin in *Shakespearian Romance* (1972). Another interpretation of Romance is explored by Northrop Frye in *The Anatomy of Criticism* (1957), *A Natural Perspective. The Development of Shakespearian Comedy and Romance* (1965), and in his introduction to the Pelican edition of *The Tempest*, where the comedies and late plays are drawn together as expressions of 'the great rising rhythms of life: marriage, springtime, harvest, dawn, and rebirth' (Pelican Introduction, p. 26). Frye traces through these plays a pattern or movement by which the characters leave restricting court society, live for a time in a 'green world' where they undergo experiences of 'chaos, tempest, illusion, madness, darkness, death' to be associated with 'a phase of confused identity', and emerge purgatorially cleansed and newly responsive to their place in the cycle of nature. An association between the late plays and seasonal mythology has been made by a number of critics in this century, particularly in relation to *The Winter's Tale*, which lends itself very readily to the idea of a vegetational myth of rebirth, both in its treatment of parents and children and its overt seasonal references; *The Tempest* fits this pattern less conveniently, but it is not at all difficult to find many kinds of images of renewal in it, from the religious terminology of Ariel's 'three men of sin' speech, to the blessings of Ceres on the marriage of Ferdinand and Miranda, and the Boatswain's description of his miraculously repaired vessel at the play's end.

In fact, *The Tempest*, as Anne Righter says in the introduction to the Penguin edition, 'is an extraordinarily obliging work of art. It will lend itself to almost any interpretation, any set of meanings imposed upon it' (p. 22). It is a play which has not only stimulated a multiplicity of interpretations and criticism but has also inspired a considerable range of other works of literature. The earliest is John Fletcher's play *The Sea Voyage* (1622), which borrows from Shakespeare the opening storm, the desert island setting, and the character of the woman who has been brought up without ever seeing a man. Soon afterwards the storm and the Miranda-like girl reappeared in another play, *The Goblins* (1638), by Sir John Suckling. Milton was influenced in *Comus* by *The Tempest*'s blend of masque and dramatic form, as well as by its magical atmosphere; some of Ariel's qualities are found in both the Attendant Spirit and in Comus himself, and Prospero's white magic is perverted into Comus's black arts. The enchanted banquet in Act III of *The Tempest* is recalled in *Paradise Regained* Book II, where Christ, like Alonso and the courtiers, is tempted by an illusory feast which disappears 'with sound of harpies' wings'. The most famous play derived from *The Tempest* is of course the adaptation by Dryden and Davenant, subtitled *The Enchanted Island* and produced in 1667, which itself gave rise to a whole sub-genre of imitations. Dryden and Davenant make many changes, including the provision of sisters for Miranda and Caliban, and a spirit consort for Ariel; a new made character, Hippolyto, is invented, a man who has never seen a woman, thus supplying a counterpart to Miranda and a lover for her sister, Dorinda. The neo-classical symmetry, and the permutations on the theme of natural sexuality permitted by the additional characters of Dorinda and Hippolyto, made this version very popular, and it held the stage until the nineteenth century, supplanting Shakespeare's original. Several operatic versions were based on it, beginning with one by Thomas Shadwell in 1674, which includes a chorus of devils tormenting the courtiers and ends with a spectacular masque of sea-gods. Purcell wrote the music for a revival in 1690–91, and Garrick did a production in 1756 which contained no fewer than thirty-two songs and duets and was described by a contemporary as '*The Tempest* castrated into an opera'. The success of Shadwell's opera at Dorset Gardens provoked the rival theatre company to put on a burlesque version by Thomas Duffett at the Theatre Royal, Drury Lane, in the same year. This coarse and ingenious piece, *The Mock Tempest, or The Enchanted Castle*, is set in Bridewell, a workhouse prison for convicted prostitutes, run by Prospero, where Miranda and Dorinda work as part-time whores, and Ariel as a pickpocket. But perhaps the most extraordinary of all *The Tempest*'s dramatic offspring is the sequel written by the Victorian dramatist F. G. Waldron in 1797, entitled *The Virgin Queen*. In this play the action takes place during the journey of Shakespeare's characters back to Milan; Caliban conspires with Antonio and Sebastian against Prospero, and even Claribel, and her husband King Abdullah of Tunis, with whom the company is by happy coincidence united, are impotent to help him. Ariel eventually saves the situation by retrieving Prospero's magic staff and book from the depths of the sea, and this time Caliban, Antonio and Sebastian get left behind when the rest set sail for home.

The Tempest has had its influence on non-dramatic literature too. Shelley impersonated Ariel in his verse address to Jane Williams entitled 'Ariel to Miranda', and Browning composed a verse monologue for Caliban, meditating on the nature of God in 'Caliban upon Setebos'. In more recent times, T. S. Eliot alluded to the play in *The Waste Land* and W. H. Auden wrote a long work, partly in a range of verse forms and partly in prose, entitled *The Sea and the Mirror*, which is the most creative and suggestive of all commentaries on the play. In this work, each of Shakespeare's characters speaks in turn, using a different kind of verse, to express his or her own nature and by implication offer an interpretation of Shakespeare's meaning. Prospero, for instance, speaks as the retiring artist, bidding farewell to Ariel, who represents not only his creativity but also his spiritual side. Auden's main character, however, is Caliban, whose speech is singled out from the rest by both length and style; it consists of an extensive and difficult prose passage, modelled on the later writing of Henry James, thus countermanding in its intellectual subtlety Shakespeare's conception of a simple semi-bestial being. For Auden, Caliban represents the physicality of life which Prospero, abetted by Ariel, has unwisely neglected and suppressed. Auden makes Caliban conspicuously eloquent and persuasive in order to show that there is a real alternative to the view of the relationship of art and life represented by Prospero and Ariel; and, paradoxically, Caliban is also made the mouthpiece for a Christian viewpoint, that the real function of art is, by its own imperfection, to represent to the audience or reader their condition of estrangement from the truth, 'to make you unforgettably conscious of the ungarnished offended gap between what you so questionably are and what you are commanded without any question to become'. Auden sees Prospero's attempt to impose order on his world as a failure; not only is it evaded by Caliban but it is subverted by Antonio, who comments mockingly on the speeches of all the other characters to show how he remains outside Prospero's charmed circle:

> *Your all is partial, Prospero;*
> *My will is all my own:*
> *Your need to love shall never know*
> *Me: I am I, Antonio,*
> *By choice myself alone.*

Aldous Huxley in his novel *Brave New World* used the play as a basis for his satiric vision of the future; the 'brave new world' admired by Miranda is in fact a hideous technocratic society where all the inhabitants, purged of their notions of family, feelings or individuality, live out their lives according to their programming, as Alpha-plus scientists or Epsilon-quality morons. John, a 'savage' from a reservation in Mexico where people still live in old-style communities, who has learnt to read from an ancient copy of Shakespeare, comes innocently to the new world in search of his father. But, unlike Miranda, he is horrified by what he learns of mankind and civilization, and the book ends with his suicide.

Sources

One can divide the sources of *The Tempest* into three classes: those where verbal resemblance shows that Shakespeare referred to them specifically for speeches in his play; those where similarities of theme or plot are so close as to suggest direct influence; and those where there are correspondences of a more generalized kind, in language, theme, or subject, which may imply much, but can prove nothing certain. It is, of course, important to remember that no single work has ever been found to account for the origin of *The Tempest* and its plot as a whole, although we know it to have been Shakespeare's common practice to take his stories from other literary works, such as Italian *novelle*, contemporary narrative poems or prose, or chronicle histories.

In the first category of source-material come three works: William Strachey's pamphlet *A True Reportory of the Wrack* (written 1610, published 1625), John Florio's translation of Montaigne's Essay 'Of the Canniballes' (1603), and Arthur Golding's translation of Ovid's *Metamorphoses* (1567). Strachey's pamphlet is one of several dealing with the colonizing expedition of Sir Thomas Gates to Virginia in 1609 and the wreck of his flagship, the Sea-Adventure, off the coast of Bermuda, and it is more than likely that Shakespeare read others, particularly Sylvester Jourdain's *Discovery of the Bermudas* (1610) and the *True Declaration of the Estate of the Colony in Virginia* (1610), published by the Council of Virginia. These pamphlets as a group are such a significant source for *The Tempest* that it is hard to deal with them separately; verbal links are evident only with Strachey's pamphlet, but it is clearly the subject matter and moral ideas behind the pamphlets which influence *The Tempest*, rather than phrases or images, and in this regard they are all very similar.

Shakespeare was inspired in a general way by the story of this voyage, which was still topical when *The Tempest* was first performed, and he may even have known William Strachey personally. The fleet set out from London in May 1609, the largest colonizing expedition ever from England, nine vessels and six hundred passengers. The Sea-Adventure, with Sir Thomas Gates and Strachey on board, was separated from the other vessels and driven off-course in a hurricane to the 'dangerous and dreaded Iland, or rather Ilands of Bermudas ... called commonly, The Devils Ilands, ... feared and avoided of all sea travellers alive' (G. Bullough, ed.,

Narrative and Dramatic Sources of Shakespeare, London and New York, 1975, Vol. VIII, 280). Everyone expected to die in the violence of the storm, 'in which the sea swelled above the Clouds and gave battell unto Heaven. It could not be said to raine, the waters like whole Rivers did flood in the ayre' (Bullough, pp. 276–7), and once the ship had sprung a leak they gave up all hope. But miraculously they survived, bailing out water ceaselessly for four days, throwing quantities of luggage and butts of beer, cider and wine overboard, inspired by Sir George Somers, Admiral of the Fleet, to toil without sleep or food. When they had reached the limits of their endurance, as Strachey saw it, God rewarded their labours:

> *It being now Friday, the fourth morning, it wanted little, but that there had bin a general determination, to have shut up hatches, and commending our sinfull soules to God, committed the Shippe to the mercy of the sea: surely, that night we must have done it, and that night had we then perished: but see the goodnesse and sweet introduction of better hope, by our mercifull God given unto us. Sir George Summers, when no man dreamed of such happinesse, had discovered, and cried Land.*

(Bullough, p. 279)

They ran the ship aground less than a mile offshore, and landed everyone safely. Good fortune continued and the Bermudas turned out to be quite other than expected. As the author of *A True Declaration of the Estate of the Colonie in Virginia* (1610) put it:

> *The Islands of the Bermudas have ever been accounted as an inchaunted pile of rockes and desert inhabitation for Divels; but all the Fairies of the Rocks were but flocks of birds, and all the Divels that haunted the woods, were but heards of swine.*

(Bullough, p. 296)

The Colonists found abundant wild life, particularly of birds, turtles and wild hogs, and fresh water, though none of the springs mentioned in *The Tempest*, yet despite all this evidence of God's providential mercy, things still did not go smoothly. A mutinous group broke off from the main body, and conspired to undermine the project, led by Somers, to build a boat and make preparations for sailing to Virginia in the spring. The rebels, according to Strachey, were motivated by laziness and the spirit of anarchy. They wanted a life of lawless ease, like that which Gonzalo describes in his ideal commonwealth in *The Tempest* (II.1.150–68), and wanted to stay on in the Bermudas rather than make the effort of getting to Virginia. One band of mutineers was discovered trying to spread discontent and sedition, and banished 'to an Iland farre by it selfe'

(Bullough, p. 288); another group, led by a discontented gentleman named Henry Paine, even planned to murder the governor and take over the island for themselves, as Caliban encourages Stephano to do, but in the event the plans were not carried out and Paine was executed. All this dissension in the face of the valiant efforts of Somers and Gates to keep order in their band and carry out their mission to proceed to Virginia causes Strachey to meditate with some gloom on human fallibility and the need for strong authoritarian rule:

> *In these dangers and divellish disquiets (whilest the almighty God wrought for us, and sent us miraculously delivered from the calamities of the Sea, all blessings upon the shoare, to content and binde us to gratefulnesse) thus inraged amongst our selves, to the destruction each of other, into what a mischiefe and misery had wee bin given up, had wee not had a Governor with his authority, to have suppressed the same?*

(Bullough, p. 289)

However, they survived the winter, which was mild, managed to build two small ships, with Somers taking an active part to encourage the labour (see Passage 1, p. 88), and in them sailed to Jamestown, Virginia, in May 1610 to join up with the remainder of the expedition. The story does not end there, for the colonists on the other vessels who had not been caught up in the storm but reached their appointed destination on time had fared much less well once they arrived. During the winter more than three hundred of the original four hundred had died, of famine and disease. With no strong leadership from men like Gates and Somers they had been unable to organize a community; there was no order and no cooperation:

> *Every man overvaluing his own worth, would be a Commander; every man underprising an others value, denied to be commanded.*

(*A True Declaration*, Bullough, p. 297)

The chroniclers of the expedition were at one in seeing the fate of this settlement as evidence, not of the folly of colonialist enterprise as such, as certain modern supporters of Caliban's position in *The Tempest* might have wished, but rather as sure proof of how no venture can profit without human labour and effort; nature will not provide of its own benison alone. As the author of *A True Declaration* wrote:

> *A Colony is therefore denominated, because they should be Coloni, the Tillers of the Earth, and Stewards of fertilitie: our mutinous loyterers would not sow with providence, and therefore they reaped the fruits of too deere bought Repentance ... Dei laboribus omnia vendunt, God sels all things for*

our labour, when Adam himself might not live in Paradice without dressing the Garden.

(quoted from F. Kermode, ed., *The Tempest*, Arden edition, 1954)

In the end Somers too died in the Bermudas, but Gates came back to England in September 1610, and travelling with him was Sylvester Jourdain, who promptly published his *Discovery of the Bermudas* in October, so the whole story was out.

As can be seen there was much raw material of several kinds here for Shakespeare; the influence of the description of the storm and shipwreck is immediately obvious, one of the clearest borrowings being from Strachey's account of the appearance of St Elmo's fire to the mariners (see Passage 2, p. 88), which inspired Ariel's speech (I.2.195–206). But the moral themes strongly stressed in Strachey and the other pamphlets are equally important. The 'providence divine', to which Prospero ascribes his own good fortune in landing safely on the island with Miranda, and to which Gonzalo appeals ('For it is you that have chalk'd forth the way/Which brought us hither'), is the power which delivers the voyagers from almost certain death in the storm and has them cast ashore on a fertile island. But the impact of divine benevolence on human life is tempered by the innate propensity to treachery and to rebellion against authority in the hearts of many, like Antonio and Caliban's fellow conspirators in *The Tempest*. As Strachey says repeatedly, the imperfections of human nature work against the goodness of God, and in many situations men naturally behave badly rather than well. Perhaps some of the reasons why *The Tempest*'s vision of life is less consoling than that in the other romances may be found in the influence of the voyagers' pamphlets.

Florio's translation of Montaigne's Essay 'Of the Canniballes' (Book 1, Chapter xxx) came out in 1603, six years before the Virginia expedition, and is another important source both verbally and thematically for Shakespeare's play. Montaigne too was interested in the colonizing of North America, and obtained information for his essay from a servant who had spent some years there. He had read earlier colonial literature also known to Shakespeare, such as Sebastian Münster's *Cosmographia Universalis*, in which Amerigo Vespucci's encounters with the native inhabitants are described. His essay contrasts the corrupt civilization of the Old World with the natural and innocent society of the New; the customs and habits of cannibals, he says, are barbaric only by our over-sophisticated standards, and to a true-sighted and objective judge represent an ideal of pure simplicity even finer than that of the legendary Golden Age.

I am sorie, Lycurgus *and* Plato *had it not* [i.e., knowledge of the North American Indians]: *for me seemeth that what in those nations we see by experience, dost not only exceed all the pictures wherewith licentious Poesie hath proudly imbellished the golden age, and all her quaint inventions to faine a happy condition of men, but also the conception and desire of Philosophy. They could not imagine a genuitie* [simplicity] *so pure and simple, as we see it by experience: nor ever beleeve our societie might be maintained with so little art and humane combination.*

(Montaigne, Essays, Everyman edn, Vol. 1, p. 220)

This view finds its place in *The Tempest*, but used in an indirect way, in Act II, Scene 1, where Gonzalo, attempting in the kindness of his heart to distract Alonso from grieving over the loss of his son, creates a fantasy vision of how he would rule the island if it were his to govern. His phrasing in several places exactly echoes that of Florio's translation (see Passage 3, p. 89):

> *I 'th' commonwealth I would by contraries*
> *Execute all things. For* no kind of traffic
> *Would I admit,* no name of magistrate.
> *Letters should not be known.* Riches, poverty,
> And use of service, none. Contract, succession,
> *Bourn, bound of land, tilth, vineyard, none.*
> No use of metal, corn, or wine, *or oil.*
> *No occupation:* all men idle, all,
> *And women too, but innocent and pure.*
> *No sovereignty –*

(II.1.150–59)

It is interesting that in the second part of Gonzalo's speech, which continues after sarcastic asides by Sebastian and Antonio, his imaginary commonwealth becomes noticeably more idealized than Montaigne's description:

> *All things in common nature should produce*
> *Without sweat or endeavour. Treason, felony,*
> *Sword, pike, knife, gun, or need of any engine*
> *Would I not have; but nature should bring forth*
> *Of its own kind all foison, all abundance,*
> *To feed my innocent people.*

(II.1.163–8)

Although Montaigne's Indians live in a fertile and temperate climate and spend most of their time drinking or dancing, he does not stress the effortless ease of their life as Gonzalo does; moreover, the Indians are a warlike people, and even though they may have no 'pike, knife, gun' or metal weapon, they fight vigorously with bows and wooden swords against neighbouring peoples: 'It is an admirable thing to see the constant resolution of their combats, which never end but by effusion of bloud and murther: for they know not what feare or rowts [retreats] are' (Montaigne, *Essays*, Everyman edn, Vol. 1, p. 223).

The context of Gonzalo's speeches provides an important perspective. We know from Prospero's account of his banishment from Milan that Gonzalo, 'a noble Neapolitan', has done his best to make the island exile more tolerable by providing some luxuries and, in particular, books, so that we already conceive of him as virtuous and well intentioned, if perhaps a little ineffectual; and his efforts to console Alonso certainly bear out this impression. Sebastian and Antonio, on the other hand, are already clearly the villains, and their cynical witticisms in this scene, always at someone else's expense, do not endear them to an audience. But though they are corrupt they are not stupid; and their jibes at Gonzalo do not fail to expose the illogicalities in his Utopian conception. These things, together with the portrayal of Caliban, the 'natural man' in the play, make it evident that although Shakespeare took Montaigne's position into account in his treatment of the relationship of civilization and nature in *The Tempest* he did not construct his play so as to endorse it. But neither does he entirely reject it: conditioned also by the very different attitude of the voyagers' pamphlets towards nature and virtue, *The Tempest* presents us not only with the grossly bestial Caliban, who has rejected or subverted the civilizing overtures of Prospero, but also with the degradation and corruption of those courtiers and their servants who have enjoyed the advantages of civilized society. Unlike Montaigne, Shakespeare does not judge; it is one of the qualities of his rich and large-souled genius that he can present a complex issue in so rounded and open a way.

Another important source which influences both the language and the themes of *The Tempest* is Ovid's *Metamorphoses*, Book VII. *Metamorphoses* is one of the seminal works behind all of Shakespeare's writing and seems to have been part of the furniture of his mind from his earliest days. He would probably have used a heavily annotated text of Ovid in Latin, containing a mass of learned commentary and allegorical interpretation, as well as the contemporary translation by Arthur Golding, published in 1567. He had already drawn on Book VII for *A Midsummer Night's Dream*, a play which in its treatment of magic has so many significant resemblances to *The Tempest*, using the favourite episode of Medea's conjuring which is referred to in *Macbeth* as well as *The Tempest*. Ovid's world of fantasy and shape-changing is a persuasive influence on *The Tempest*, on, for instance, the mercurial Ariel, and the natural forms of the island, differently perceived according to the temperament of the beholder, as well as on the grotesquerie of Caliban and the spirits conjured up by Prospero. Both Ovid and Shakespeare celebrate the poignant beauty of evanescent appearances. Ovid's grandest vision of human life in terms of a constant process of change is expressed in *Metamorphoses* Book XV through the mouth of the philosopher Pythagoras, widely revered in the Renaissance as sage and promulgator of the doctrine of the transmigration of souls. As one might expect, Ovid uses images from the natural world, especially of seasonal change, of the shifting relationships between the elements, and of the growth, maturation, and decay of the human body at its various stages of development to embody his conception; as has often been noticed, Shakespeare is directly influenced by these images in his sonnets. Ovid also draws several times on the image of the sea as both agent and example of change at its most awesome and mysterious:

> *For my part, considering how the generations of men have passed from the age of gold to that of iron, how often the fortunes of different places have been reversed, I should believe that nothing lasts under the same form. I have seen what once was solid earth now changed into sea, and lands created out of what once was ocean. Sea shall lie far away from ocean's waves, and ancient anchors have been found on mountain tops.*
> (*Metamorphoses* XV, 257–62, trans. M. M. Innes, Penguin Classics, 1955)

To read this most poetic of all the books of Ovid's poems in conjunction with *The Tempest* is an immensely suggestive experience, even if no specific verbal parallels can be found. But there is no doubt that the very wording of Medea's incantation from Book VII, in Golding's translation, is behind Prospero's resonant soliloquy in Act V, Scene 1, in which he bids farewell to his magic arts (see Passage 4, p. 90):

> Ye elves of hills, brooks, *standing lakes, and groves,*
> *And ye that on the sands with printless foot*
> *Do chase the ebbing Neptune, and do fly him*
> *When he comes back; you demi-puppets that*
> *By moonshine do the green, sour ringlets make,*
> *Whereof the ewe not bites; and you whose pastime*
> *Is to make midnight mushrumps, that rejoice*
> *To hear the solemn curfew,* by whose aid –

> *Weak masters though ye be* – I have bedimmed
> The noontide sun, *called forth the mutinous winds,*
> *And 'twixt the green sea and the azured vault*
> *Set roaring war; to the dread rattling thunder*
> *Have I given fire, and rifted Jove's stout oak*
> *With his own bolt; the strong-based promontory*
> *Have I made shake, and by the spurs plucked up*
> *The pine and cedar; graves at my command*
> *Have waked their sleepers, oped, and let 'em forth*
> *By my so potent art.*
>
> (V.1.33–50)

In Ovid, the words form part of an incantation to the demons spoken by the witch Medea when she is trying by magic to prolong the life of her lover Jason's father, Aeson. In commentaries on Ovid current in Shakespeare's time, Medea was seen as an exponent of black magic; her arts were much more akin to those of Sycorax than of Prospero, and in the speech which Shakespeare adapts she is calling upon the spirits of nature to give her the power to commit an unnatural act. Accordingly, Shakespeare modifies her language for Prospero, and although the speech mingles the sinister and the domestic aspects of the supernatural, the dimming of the sun and the waking of the dead on one hand, the dainty elves who create fairy rings and make mushrooms grow overnight on the other, the tone is much less ominous. Even so the speech stresses the extraordinary powers Prospero has acquired over the natural world, and the reference to 'heavenly music' which he calls for at the end of it perhaps implies that Prospero's abandoning of his 'rough magic' is a welcome retreat from a world of danger and mystery.

Another likely source for *The Tempest*, including a few details of language, is Ben Jonson's Masque *Hymenaei*, written to celebrate the marriage of the Earl of Essex to Frances, daughter of the Earl of Suffolk, and performed at the old Banqueting House in Whitehall, in January 1606. The verbal echoes are not extensive or close, but they do exist; Prospero's 'Our revels now are ended' speech (IV.1.148–58) is influenced by Jonson's prefatory remarks on the ephemerality of masque spectacle (see Passage 5, p. 91) and it also seems possible that the conclusion of this passage ('I am contented, those fastidious *stomachs* should leave my full tables, and enjoy at home, their cleane empty trenchers, fittest for such airy tastes') is recalled in the scene of the vanishing banquet (III.3). Other connections are with the betrothal masque in *The Tempest*. In Jonson's masque, premarital chastity is strongly stressed, and Venus as a force subordinated to the twin powers of Hymen and Juno; Juno appears in her role as goddess of marriage attended by Iris in a rainbow-coloured costume. Jonson provides elaborate descriptions of the costumes and of the sets (see Passage 6, p. 92) as realized by Inigo Jones, and though such splendour and spectacle could not be reproduced for a Globe production of *The Tempest* it could have been imitated for performances at Court or at the Blackfriars Theatre.

There are many other literary and dramatic works with intriguing similarities to various aspects of *The Tempest*, though in most cases there is no evidence to indicate a relationship other than that of analogy or generalized influence. Certain contemporary plays, for instance, contain elements which may throw some light on how particular characters or scenes in Shakespeare's play might have been regarded at the time. In the anonymous popular romance *Mucedorus* (*c*. 1590), which was specially revived for performance in 1610, there is a villainous Wild Man called Bremo, armed with a cudgel, who threatens to kill the heroine, Amadine, and then, overcome by the mysterious power of her virginity, falls in love with her and attempts to woo her; eventually he is slain in a comic scene by Mucedorus, a Prince disguised as a shepherd and, of course, Amadine's real lover. This isn't much like the Caliban–Miranda–Ferdinand relationship, but Shakespeare had probably used *Mucedorus*, which features a wild bear, for *The Winter's Tale*, and the crude Wild Man Bremo may have been a prototype for the much more subtly portrayed Caliban. In *John a Kent and John a Cumber* (1594), by Anthony Munday, there is a Welsh magician, John a Kent, who uses his arts to promote the causes of virtue and true love; he has an attendant spirit called Shrimp who assists him by playing sweet music with which he consoles the two young heroines, Sydanen and Marian, putting them to sleep with music, to the amazement of the other characters present on stage, and later distracts them from following the girls by devious tricks. The uses of magic and music here are very reminiscent of Ariel, and so too is the situational humour whereby the audience can see Shrimp and his trickery, but for the characters on stage he is invisible.

Perhaps more significant and also more elusive than either of these English plays is the Italian *Commedia dell' arte*. Shakespeare could have known of this dramatic tradition, which is dependent on largely extemporized dialogue devised to meet the demands of a given plot or situation, either through the visits of Italian players to England in the 1570s or through the general fund of knowledge about 'extemporal' drama to which there are so many references in Elizabethan plays. Several *scenarii* for *Commedia dell' arte* plays have been discovered which bear more than a passing resemblance to the plot of *The Tempest.* In *Li Tre Satiri (The Three Satyrs),* for instance, there is a magician served by spirits in the shape of wild men, a virginal girl, Phillis, who falls in love for the first time, a storm and shipwreck, and clowns who dress up in stolen garments. Two of the shipwrecked mariners steal the magician's book and conjure with it. The magician, a very equivocal figure in this play, imprisons all the characters within a magic circle until his book is returned to him; the story ends happily, with the discovery by one of the shipwrecked mariners of his long lost son, who is then married to the virginal Phillis. In other scenarii there are magicians both good and evil, and in *Arcadia Incantata* one who conjures up a storm and gets his spirits to torment the shipwrecked mariners. Parallels of this kind can be multiplied almost indefinitely, but since there is no proof that Shakespeare ever actually witnessed a *Commedia dell' arte* performance no specific influence can be claimed. A comedy written in German by Jacob Ayrer of Nuremberg, *Die Schöne Sidea (The Fair Sidea),* and extant in an English translation of 1618 has many tantalizing analogies with *The Tempest,* including a Duke banished from his lands who practises magic, a resentful devil servant, a daughter who falls in love with the son of her father's enemy, and a scene where this young man is made to chop logs to please her; but again, nothing can be proved, and the temperate view of Bullough, in *Narrative and Dramatic Sources of Shakespeare,* is the wisest attitude:

> Die Schöne Sidea *throws little light on Shakespeare's play, but it supports the conclusion that behind* The Tempest *there was a large international body of folklore and romantic tradition.*

> (Vol. VIII, p. 249)

Many non-dramatic sources in narrative prose have also been suggested, including certain Spanish prose romances of the sixteenth century, but the one romance which is most seminal is the pastoral romance of the Hellenistic Greek writer Longus, *Daphnis and Chloe,* the archetypal story of young love developing between an innocent couple living on an island completely untouched by urban civilization. It has been demonstrated that not only is *Daphnis and Chloe* the ultimate source for the chief elements in a style of pastoral plot used by Sidney in *Arcadia,* by Spenser in Book Six of *The Faerie Queene,* and by Shakespeare in *As You Like It, Cymbeline* and *The Winter's Tale,* but also that *The Tempest* itself has several correspondences both general and specific and possible verbal parallels with an Elizabethan translation of it available to Shakespeare. In *Daphnis and Chloe* and in *The Tempest* innocence, youth and island isolation are central features in the love stories; there are correspondences between the characters of the two young men Daphnis and Ferdinand, and the two maidens Chloe and Miranda, particularly in the sexual innocence of the latter and the fact that although they have been brought up in the pastoral world they are both in actuality of high birth. There is a structural counterpart to Prospero in *Daphnis and Chloe* in the character of Philetus, a wise old herdsman who presides over the love affair; he is the only one able to see the god Eros, who functions as a partly allegorical character and, like Ariel, brings the lovers together. In both works nymphs and reapers appear in a ceremony to honour the lovers and bless their union. It has also been noticed (by Carol Gesner, in 'The Tempest as Pastoral Romance', *Shakespeare Quarterly*, X, 1959) that a passage from the translation by Angel Day, published in 1587, contains a whole collocation of phrases which reappear in similar forms at various points in the play (see Passage 7, p. 92), particularly in the scene of the vanishing banquet. In this passage Longus describes a supernatural commotion caused by the god Pan, protector of the island community, in outrage at a band of foreigners from the mainland who have landed on the island to raid and plunder, and to kidnap Chloe. Pan appears in a vision to the Captain of those marauders to reprove them and demand Chloe's return. The Captain, struck with wonder, complies at once. Though the circumstances differ, this scene bears important similarities to Act III, Scene 3 of *The Tempest* where Ariel appears to Alonso and his company to terrify them and awaken their conscience. The elements of a storm at sea, strange and magical sounds and appearances, human terror, and divine anger at mortal misdeeds, occur in both works. It can be seen that the influence of Longus, and perhaps the phrasing of Day, extend considerably further than the pastoral aspects of Shakespeare's play to areas where their appearance is much more surprising.

Shakespeare's use of source-material in *The Tempest* testifies to his typical eclecticism of method, and to the extraordinary synthesizing power of his imagination. The play is resonant with literary echoes of many kinds; and though it is not always helpful to search out evidence for specific influences, there is no doubt that the play grows in richness from its multifarious associations.

Passage 1

In the meane space did one Frubbusher ... (a painefull and well experienced Shipwright, and skilfull workman) labour the building of a little Pinnace: for the furtherance of which, the Governour dispensed with no travaile of his body, nor forbare any care or study of minde, perswading (as much and more, an ill qualified parcell of people, by his owne performance, then by authority, thereby to hold them at their worke, namely to fell, carry, and sawe Cedar, fit for the Carpenters purpose (for what was so meane, whereto he would not himselfe set his hand, being therefore up earely and downe late?) yet neverthelesse were they hardly drawne to it, as the Tortoise to the inchantment, as the Proverbe is, but his owne presence and hand being set to every meane labour, and imployed so readily to every office, made our people at length more diligent, and willing to be called thereunto, where, they should see him before they came. In which, we may observe how much example prevailes above precepts, and how readier men are to be led by eyes, then eares.

And sure it was happy for us, who had now runne this fortune, and were fallen into the bottome of this misery, that we both had our Governour with us, and one so solicitous and carefull, whose both example (as I said) and authority, could lay shame, and command upon our people: else, I am perswaded, we had most of us finished our dayes there, so willing were the major part of the common sort (especially when they found such a plenty of victuals) to settle a foundation of ever inhabiting there; as well appeared by many practises of theirs (and perhaps of some of the better sort). Loe, what are our affections and passions, if not rightly squared? how irreligious, and irregular they expresse us? not perhaps so ill as we would be, but yet as wee are; some dangerous and secret discontents nourished among us, had like to have bin the parents of bloudy issues and mischiefes.

From W. Strachey, *The Wracke and Redemption of Sir Thomas Gates* (1610)

Passage 2

During all this time, the heavens look'd so blacke upon us, that it was not possible the elevation of the Pole might be observed: nor a Starre by night, nor Sunne beame by day was to be seene. Onely upon the Thursday night Sir George Summers being upon the watch, had an apparition of a little round light, like a faint Starre, trembling, and streaming along with a sparkeling blaze, halfe the height upon the Maine Mast, and shooting sometimes from Shroud to Shroud, tempting to settle as it were upon any of the foure Shrouds: and for three or foure hours together, or rather more, halfe the night it kept with us; running sometimes along the Maine-yard to the very end, and then returning. At which, Sir George Summers called divers about him, and shewed them the same, who observed it with much wonder, and carefulnesse: but upon a sodaine, towards the morning watch, they lost the sight of it, and knew not what way it made. The superstitious Sea-men make many constructions of this Sea-fire, which neverthlesse is usuall in stormes: the same (it may be) which the Graecians were wont in the Mediterranean to call Castor and

Pollux, of which, if one onely appeared without the other, they tooke it for an evill signe of great tempest. The Italians, and such, who lye open to the Adriatique and Tyrrene Sea, call it (a sacred Body) Corpo sancto: the Spaniards call it Saint Elmo, and have an authentique and miraculous Legend for it. Be it what it will, we laid other foundations of safety or ruine, then in the rising or falling of it, but could it have served us now miraculously to have taken our height by, it might have strucken amazement, and a reverence in our devotions, according to the due of a miracle.

From W. Strachey, *The Wracke and Redemption of Sir Thomas Gates* (1610)

Passage 3

The lawes of nature doe yet command them, which are but little bastardized by ours, And that with such puritie, as I am sometimes grieved the knowledge of it came no sooner to light, at what time there were men, that better than we could have judged of it. I am sorie, *Lycurgus* and *Plato* had it not: for me seemeth that what in those nations we see by experience, doth not only exceed all the pictures wherewith licentious Poesie hath proudly imbellished the golden age, and all her quaint inventions to faine a happy condition of man, but also the conception and desire of Philosophy. They could not imagine a genuitie so pure and simple, as we see it by experience; nor ever beleeve our societie might be maintained with so little art and humane combination. It is a nation, would I answer *Plato*, that hath no kinde of traffike, no knowledge of Letters, no intelligence of numbers, no name of magistrate, nor of politike superioritie; no use of service, of riches or of povertie; no contracts, no successions, no partitions, no occupation but idle; no respect of kinred, but common, no apparell but naturall, no manuring of lands, no use of wine, corne, or mettle. The very words that import lying, falsehood, treason, dissimulations, covetousnes, envie, detraction, and pardon, were never heard of amongst them. How dissonant would hee finde his imaginarie commonwealth from this perfection!

> *Hos natura modos primum dedit.*

> Nature at first uprise,
> These manners did devise.

Furthermore, they live in a country of so exceeding pleasant and temperate situation, that as my testimonies have told me, it is verie rare to see a sicke body amongst them; and they have further assured me, they never saw any man there, either shaking with the palsie, toothlesse, with eies dropping, or crooked and stooping through age.

From Montaigne, *Essayes*, 'Of the Canniballes', translated by J. Florio (1603)

Passage 4

The starres alonly faire and bright did in the welkin shine.
To which she lifting up hir handes did thrise hirselfe encline,
And thrice with water of the brooke hir haire besprincled shee:
And gasping thrise she opte hir mouth: and bowing downe hir knee
Upon the bare hard ground, she said: O trustie time of night
Most faithfull unto privities, O golden starres whose light
Doth jointly with the Moone succeede the beames that blaze by day
And thou three headed *Hecate* who knowest best the way
To compasse this our great attempt and art our chiefest stay:
Ye Charmes and Witchcrafts, and thou Earth which both with herbe and weed
Of mightie working furnishest the Wizardes at their neede:
Ye Ayres and windes: ye Elves of Hilles, of Brookes, of Woods alone,
Of standing Lakes, and of the Night approche ye everychone.
Through helpe of whom (the crooked bankes much wondring at the thing)
I have compelled streames to run cleane backward to their spring.
By charmes I make the calme Seas rough, and make the rough Seas plaine
And cover all the Skie with Cloudes, and chase them thence againe.
By charmes I rayse and lay the windes, and burst the Vipers jaw,
And from the bowels of the Earth both stones and trees doe drawe.
Whole woods and Forestes I remove: I make the Mountaines shake,
And even the Earth it selfe to grone and fearfully to quake.
I call up dead men from their graves: and thee O lightsome Moone
I darken oft, though beaten brasse abate thy perill soone.
Our Sorcerie dimmes the Morning faire, and darkes the Sun at Noone.
The flaming breath of firie Bulles ye quenched for my sake,
And caused there unwieldie neckes the bended yoke to take.
Among the Earthbred brothers you a mortall war did set
And brought asleepe the Dragon fell whose eyes were never shet.
By meanes wherof deceiving him that had the golden fleece
In charge of keepe, you sent it thence by Jason into Greece.
Now have I neede of herbes that can by vertue of their juice
To flowring prime of lustie youth old withred age reduce.
I am assurde ye will it graunt.

From Ovid, *Metamorphoses*, Book VII, 254–86, translated by A. Golding (1567)

The following is a modern English translation of this passage by M. M. Innes,
Ovid, *Metamorphoses*, Penguin Classics, 1955:

Only the stars, unresting, sparkled in the sky. Stretching up her arms towards
these stars, Medea turned herself about three times, three times sprinkled her head
with water drawn from the river, and three times uttered a wailing cry. Then,
sinking to her knees on the hard earth, 'O night,' she prayed, 'most faithful guardian

of my secrets, and golden stars, who, with the moon, succeed the brightness of the day, goddess Hecate, triple-formed, you who ever know my undertakings, and come to aid my spells and magic arts and you, O earth, the source of the magician's powerful herbs: you too, breezes and winds, mountains rivers and lakes, all spirits of the groves and of the night, be present! By your help I can at will turn rivers to run backwards to their source, between their astonished banks, I can soothe the stormy seas or rouse their placid surface with my songs, dispel or bring up the clouds, summon or dismiss the winds, burst open serpents with my spells and incantations: I can move living rocks and trees, making oaks uproot themselves from the soil, even whole forests; I bid the mountains tremble, the earth produce dull rumblings, and the ghosts rise from their tombs. The moon, too, I draw down from the sky, though the bronze cymbals of Temesa do their best to aid her struggles. Even my grandfather's chariot grows pale at my song, and Dawn loses her colour as a result of my potions. It was you who dulled for me the fiery breath of the bulls, and harnessed to the crooked plough those necks which had never drawn a load before. You stirred up fierce strife in the ranks of the warriors who sprang up from the serpent's teeth, you lulled to sleep the ever-wakeful dragon, and when you had tricked the guardian, sent the golden fleece of Greece. Now I have need to essences by which an old man may be restored to the flower of his youth, and regain the prime of life. And you will give me them.

Passage 5

It is a noble and just advantage, that the things subiected to *understanding* have of those which are obiected to *sense*, that the one sort are but momentarie, and meerely taking; the other impressing, and lasting: Else the glorie of all these *solemnities* had perish'd like a blaze, and gone out, in the *beholders* eyes. So short-liv'd are the *bodies* of all things, in comparison of their *soules*. And, though *bodies* oft-times have the ill luck to be sensually preferr'd, they find afterwards, the good fortune (when *soules* live) to be utterly forgotten. This it is hath made the most royall *Princes* and greatest *persons* (who are commonly the *personaters* of these *actions*) not onely studious of riches, and magnificence in the outward celebration, or shew; (which rightly becomes them) but curious after the most high and heartie *inventions*, to furnish the inward parts: (and those grounded vpon *antiquitie*, and solide *learnings*) which, though their *voyce* be taught to sound to present occasions, their *sense*, or doth, or should alwayes lay hold on more remov'd *mysteries*. And, howsoever some may squemishly crie out, that all endevour of *learning*, and *sharpness* in these transitorie *devices* expecially, where it steps beyond their little, or (let me not wrong 'hem) no braine at all, is superfluous; I am contented, these fastidious *stomachs* should leave my full tables, and enjoy at home, their cleane empty trenchers, fittest for such airy tastes . . .

From Ben Jonson, *Hymenaei, or the Solemnities of a Masque and Barriers at a Marriage* (1606)

Passage 6

Here, the upper part of the *Scene*, which was all of Clouds, and made artificially to swell, and ride like the Racke, began to open; and, the ayre clearing, in the top thereof was discovered IUNO, sitting in a Throne, supported by two beautifull *Peacockes*; her attyre rich, and like a Queene, a white Diademe on her head, from whence descended a Veyle, and that bound with a *Fascia*, of severall-coloured silkes, set with all sorts of jewels, and raysed in the top with *Lillies* and *Roses*; in her right hand she held a Scepter, in the other a timbrell, at her golden feete the hide of a lyon was placed: round about her sate the spirites of the ayre, in severall colours, making musique: Above her the region of *fire*, with a continuall motion, was seene to whirle circularly, and JUPITER standing in the toppe (figuring the *heaven*) brandishing his thunder: Beneath her the *rainebowe*, IRIS, and, on the two sides eight ladies, attired richly, and alike in the most celestiall colours, who represented her *powers*, as shee is the *governesse* of *marriage*, and made the second *masque*. All which, upon the discoverie, REASON made narration of.

From Ben Jonson, *Hymenaei, or the Solemnities of a Masque and Barriers at a Marriage* (1606)

Passage 7

... it seemed at night in the middest of their banqueting, that all the land about them was on fire, and a sodaine noise arose in their hearing as of a great fleete, and armed nauie for the seas, approching towardes them. The sound whereof and dreadfull sight, made some of the to crie *Arme Arme*, and others to gather together their companies, & weapons. One thought his fellowe next him was hurt, an other feared the shot that he heard ratling in his eares, this man thought his companion slaine hard by his side, an other seemed to stumble on dead carcasses. In briefe, the hurrie and tumult was so wonderfull and straunge, as they almost were at their wittes endes.

This great afraie continued in such sort as you haue heard all the night long, and that in so terrible manner as that they uehementlie wished for the daie, hopeing in the appearing thereof to be relieued. But yet their rest grewe not by the mornings shewe as was expected, but rather the light thereof discouered vnto them farre more fearfull and straunge effects ... A dreadful noise was heard from the rocks, not as the sound of any naturall trumpets, but far more shril and hideous, which shewed an onset to be giuen vppon them by some waighty armies. Whereof the Methimnians being in exceeding dread, hurled altogether to their weapons supposing, that the enemies from whome they had rest that spoile, had come vppon them on a sudden, without giuing them respect to gather their weapons.

By the conceit hereof may easily be gathered, howe Pan the mightie sheepheard ioining with the *Nymphes*, became aiding to their petitions, and that exercising vpon these cruell rouers, the power of a god, hee deliuered vnto their knowledge, how the mighty powers were not for some cause or other pleased with those their spoiles and robberies . . . about the middest of the day, the captaine of their galleies (not without expresse diuine prouidence) was caste in a deepe and heauie slumber. And as he lay sleeping in his cabine, to the great amaze of all the company, considering those tumules, Pan himself in a vision stoode right before him, and beeing as hee was in the shape vnder the Pine before described, he vsed vnto him these or the like speeches following.

O cruel and mischiefous sacreleger, howe haue you dared with so great and vncontrolled boldnes, in armes and shewe of war, to enter thus cruelly vppon my haunts and pastures, deare vnto me alone, as wherevpon reposeth my speciall delights . . . I heere protest and denounce vnto you, as I am the god Pan, and as the liuely flockes and heards, are vnto me of sacred pleasance, that no one of you shall euer see Methimne againe, if you do but so much as make meane to passe forwards with this pillage. Nor shall you escape the wreake of those hideous soundes that you haue heard, without leauing so much as one of you aliue, but that the sea it selfe shall soake you vppe, and your carcasses become a foode vnto the fishes: Render therefore back againe vnto the *Nymphs* their Chloe . . .

The Captaine, beeing awaked of this vision, grewe into greater feare and amaze of this heaueye charge and speeches. And calling together his soldiors and companies he caused present serch to be made for Chloe . . . Chloe was no sooner parted out of the vessel where shee was, but they heard from the hie rockes a sound againe, but nothing dreadfull as the other, but rather much sweete, melodious, and pleasing, such as the most cunning sheepheards vse before their flockes and heards, leading them vnto their pastures.

From Longus, *Daphnis and Chloe*, translated by A. Day (1587)

Suggested reading

1. Editions of *The Tempest*: New Penguin Shakespeare, ed. A. Righter, Harmondsworth, 1968. An open, suggestive introduction and lucid notes.
   The Pelican Shakespeare, ed. N. Frye, Baltimore, 1959. The introduction contains a useful expression of Frye's view of the play as myth.
   The Arden Shakespeare, ed. F. Kermode, 1954, revised and corrected 1961, 1962. Contains a terse, scholarly, excellent introduction, with particularly useful sections on Art and Nature.

2. G. Bullough, ed., *Narrative and Dramatic Sources of Shakespeare*, London and New York, 1975, Vol. VIII: The Romances. As well as providing excerpts from a dozen sources and analogues of *The Tempest*, Bullough gives a helpful account of Shakespeare's treatment of his sources for this play, and an account of Shakespeare's developing technique in the adaptation of source-material generally.

3. H. Felperin, *Shakespearian Romance*, Princeton, 1972. A wide-ranging book on the Romance mode, which supplies its background in classical and medieval literature and provides readings of the four late plays, concluding with a Bibliographical Appendix, 'The Fortunes of Romance', which traces critical attitudes towards romance from Shakespeare onwards.

4. N. Frye, *A Natural Perspective. The Development of Shakespearian Comedy and Romance*, Columbia, 1965. Four essays dealing with the comedies and late plays together, which treat the conventions of comedy and romance as non-realistic genres and interpret the plays in terms of mythical patterns. To be read in conjunction with *The Anatomy of Criticism*, Princeton, 1957, in which Frye's synoptic theory of literature is more fully described.

5. D. G. James, *The Dream of Prospero*, Oxford, 1967. A book entirely devoted to *The Tempest* which offers a Christian reading of the play and detailed chapters on the backgrounds of Renaissance magic and New World literature.

6. D. J. Palmer, ed., *Shakespeare, The Tempest. A Casebook*, London, 1968. Convenient collection of *Tempest* criticism, including excerpts

from Dryden and Davenant's adaptation of the play, the criticism of Coleridge and Dowden, and Auden's speech for Caliban from *The Sea and the Mirror*. Essays by R. A. Brower, 'The Mirror of Analogy', on the metaphorical design of the play, and R. A. Zimbardo, 'Form and Disorder in *The Tempest*', which counteracts accepted readings of the play by Tillyard and Wilson Knight, are, amongst others, given in full.

7. E. M. W. Tillyard, *Shakespeare's Last Plays*, London, 1938. An early and influential discussion of *Cymbeline, The Winter's Tale* and *The Tempest* as plays which build on and extend the vision of Shakespeare's tragedies.

8. G. Wilson Knight, *The Crown of Life. Essays in Interpretation of Shakespeare's Final Plays*, Oxford, 1947. Combines detailed discussion of the image-patterns in these plays with large-scale readings of them as life-enhancing myths celebrating reconciliation and natural harmony. Knight's account of the plays as religious works has become the basis of much later criticism. *The Shakespearian Tempest*, 1932, explores sea-imagery throughout Shakespeare's writing, with *The Tempest* as its culmination.

9. D. Young, *The Heart's Forest. A Study of Shakespeare's Pastoral Plays*, New Haven and Yale, 1972. Discusses pastoral as a Renaissance mode with treatment both of its historical background and its ethical implications, and includes chapters on *As You Like It* and *King Lear* as pastoral plays together with *The Winter's Tale* and *The Tempest*. *The Tempest*'s characteristic theatricality is also explored, as well as its relevance to the Renaissance debate about Art and Nature.